Eat, Drink, and Remarry

Eat, Drink, and Remarry

MEMORIES FROM A LIFETIME OF
ART, CLASS, AND SOUTHERN CHARM

Patricia Altschul

G

GALLERY BOOKS

New York   Amsterdam/Antwerp   London
Toronto   Sydney/Melbourne   New Delhi

Gallery Books
An Imprint of Simon & Schuster, LLC
1230 Avenue of the Americas
New York, NY 10020

First Gallery Books hardcover edition November 2025

GALLERY BOOKS and colophon are registered trademarks of Simon & Schuster, LLC

Interior design by Jaime Putorti

Manufactured in the United States of America

10 9 8 7 6 5 4 3 2 1

Library of Congress Control Number: 2025937690

ISBN 978-1-6680-6666-9
ISBN 978-1-6680-6668-3 (ebook)

For Whitney

Contents

Foreword

———◆———

Y ou might think I have a *charmed* life, where I get to sit around all day on a piazza, eyeing the world through martini-colored glasses. Guilty as charged; I love having a cocktail while relaxing on a sun-dappled lounge chair. Who doesn't? But the best thing about my life is that it has been rich in wildly diverse experiences that rarely involve being seated—and not necessarily the experiences you'd expect or even imagine.

I'm a former academic who (improbably) stars on *Southern Charm*, a reality television show. I was an art adviser who once bought and sold priceless paintings, and I'm an entrepreneur who has curated a line of affordable luxury products on the Home Shopping Network (HSN). I attended the Met Gala wearing a couture gown too voluminous to fit in a car, and I can feast at a crab boil without spilling one drop of butter on a starched white blouse. I love the finest imported caviar, but I'm equally happy with a Costco hot dog. I've been married three times but never had what most brides would call a wedding.

I enjoy—no, I *love*—being a contradiction. And I never say no to adventure. I'll give you an example.

When I was an art adviser in the 1980s, my favorite way to travel between Washington, DC, and London or Paris was the Concorde, a supersonic jet that could cross the Atlantic in three and a half hours. It was expensive, but my client was paying, and the luxury of intercontinental travel without jet lag was priceless.

On top of being sleek and swift, the Concorde was pristine. When I board a plane today, I use an antiseptic wipe to clean my seat and everything adjacent to it (I'd clean the person next to me if they'd let me) because airplanes are flying petri dishes, breeding grounds for every germ known to man, and I don't want to catch the plague. But the Concorde was so elegant that passengers actually dressed up for the occasion; blessedly, there were no flip-flops, muscle tees, exposed midriffs and navel rings, or hoodies in sight. On this occasion, I wore my favorite purple Thierry Mugler suit—a short, fitted skirt with a peplum jacket—and my highest heels. You might say I was a hot number.

Hot enough to catch the eye of the pilots, who watched as the passengers boarded. They were French, which says it all. Barbara Novak, my business partner, and I were settling into our seats when the flight attendant leaned over with an invitation. Would I like to join the pilots in the nose of the plane for takeoff? *Would I?* It sounded like an opportunity I shouldn't pass up. When she ushered me into the cockpit, I felt like I had stepped into mission control at NASA. I was greeted by three pilots, two in the front, facing a huge instrument panel, and one on the side.

The flight attendant strapped me into my seat, an understatement because it was unlike any "seat belt" I had ever seen—full body, from neck to knees. My hands were free, which was a good thing because the attendant served me champagne and caviar. While I nibbled, I had a lively conversation with the two adorable pilots in the front. They were friendly and flirtatious as they tried to explain the various dials and gauges, which made no sense to me whatsoever. The third pilot was busy preparing for what was essentially a rocket launch.

When it was time for takeoff, the flight attendant cleared my tray and gave me headphones to protect my ears from the deafening roar that would ensue. We sped down the runway for what seemed like half a second; then, we were up in the air. When the plane approached Mach 1, meaning it would be traveling at the speed of sound, I was shocked to see an opaque heat screen descend over the windshield. The pilot explained that it was protection to keep the glass from shattering. When I questioned how they would be able to see where they were going, he laughed and said, "We never see where we're going." Everything was computerized, he reassured me. The heat screen would retract when it was time to land.

During the flight, the Concorde would reach Mach 2, which is *twice* the speed of sound, so fast that, in the words of one aviation expert, "It could effectively outrun a nuclear blast and catch up with the sun." A panel in the passenger section kept track of the aircraft's speed, displaying the numbers as they ascended to Mach 1 and Mach 2.

How many people have been lucky enough to do this? I thought as I sat in the cockpit. And how wonderful that I had this amazing opportunity because life is all about highs and lows and everything in between. I found and lost love, married in haste, and, well, you know . . . survived a few near-death experiences, dined with kings, and worried about *being* dinner when I visited a tribe of Mudmen in Papua New Guinea. I've enjoyed incredible friendships with remarkable people and stayed true to myself on a reality television show, which is a real accomplishment!

My roots are in the North and the South, although I definitely identify as Southern. There should be a pronoun for *that*. When people ask me to describe the differences between the two sensibilities, I offer this explanation, which goes back to the founding of America.

In the North, the founding fathers were Pilgrims, and most were very religious. They didn't drink or smoke, and they were rigid in their social structure. They were not famous for their high spirits. In fact, they gave out scarlet letters for misbehavior.

But in the South, the founding fathers were aristocrats—gay cavaliers who loved to drink, dance, listen to music, gamble, and race horses. In other words, all the vices that one could think of were established early and have been traditions ever since. They were all about wine, women, and song, and that's what I love about the South and why I've chosen it as my home.

My album of memories is varied and full of surprises. As that charming pilot on the Concorde said, "We never see where we're going." I certainly didn't know what was ahead, but that's what has made my life so interesting. I can't wait to tell you my story.

Patricia Altschul

Eat, Drink,
and *Remarry*

One

⁓

This is not a memoir that begins with a sad tale of a deprived, Dickensian childhood. I was blessed with wonderful parents who adored their daughter—Madelyn Patricia—from the day I was born, and our life together was a great adventure.

According to family lore, my mother and father met at a cotillion in Richmond, Virginia. My mother, Frances Pearl Sudler, was a beautiful woman, polished in every way. She spoke French fluently, played the piano, and was a devotee of opera. She was skilled at needlepoint and calligraphy and an avid reader, especially poetry. She was also very intelligent. She studied nursing and radiology at Johns Hopkins and was in the Army Nurse Corps at the Walter Reed Hospital when few women had such demanding careers or *any* career.

My father, Walter Pettus Dey (pronounced "die"), was a graduate of the University of Alabama and Tulane University School of Medicine, a US Navy veteran, a surgeon, a diplomat, a world traveler, and an adventurer who had lived and worked in China and Japan in the late 1920s and early 1930s. He served as President Franklin Roosevelt's medical adviser to the Far East. He was a dashing figure in his uniform and could be found in exotic places commanding a ship (he was the first captain of the first aircraft carrier), modernizing a hospital, and saving lives.

One grateful patient gave him a small statue of a Buddha to express his gratitude. I'm fascinated by this artifact because the Buddha is hollow, and to this day I can hear something intriguing rattling inside—a diamond, a ruby, or simply dirt and rocks? Since my repeated efforts to break it open have failed, I guess I'll never know—but I'm happy imagining priceless gems!

Father retired at the age of fifty-eight and was seemingly a confirmed bachelor, the term used to describe a man who courted women but was unlikely to settle down and get married. However, he was a bit of a roué with the ladies because he was rumored to have handed out thirty engagement rings while he was single (which was most of his life). Then he met lovely Frances and was smitten. He recognized that the glamorous thirty-year-old who looked like a movie star was a sophisticated and accomplished woman who was his equal in every way. Given their medical backgrounds, they had a great deal in common.

I knew that Father's family had reservations about the match, but I grew up thinking it was because my mother, who was a Philadelphia Main Liner, had committed the unpardonable crime of being born a Yankee, something the Deys, especially my father's wildly eccentric sister, Edith, and her daughter, Edith, would consider suspicious. (Later, when I was an adult, our Big Edie and Little Edie reminded me of Jacqueline Kennedy's cousins with the same names because somehow, the house my father bought for my aunts in Florida always ended up looking dilapidated like Grey Gardens.) The family's ties to the South were strong. My grandfather Frank Edgar Dey was a brigadier general in the Confederate army, and my grandmother Carolyn Day (so she became Carolyn Day Dey, which is funny) was raised on her family's plantation in Alabama.

I consulted a genealogist who told me that in previous generations, the Dey family went all the way back to the Edict of Nantes and that they descended from a French count who married into the Dutch royal family. Later, they were colonists from England, Holland, and France who owned considerable property in New Jersey, Connecticut, and New York, including Dey Street (the site of the World Trade Center), John Street, Pearl Street, and the Bowery.

I visited the Dey mansion in Wayne, New Jersey. The Dutch Georgian house, built in the 1700s, was where George Washington and my great-great-great-grandfather plotted to defeat Cornwallis at Yorktown and win the Revolutionary War. Washington frequently housed his troops there. Even though the family was Southern through and through, the rich history of Europe, the American Revolution, and old New York were somewhere in their DNA.

My father, who was born in Texas and raised in Florida, embodied this fascinating dichotomy. He revered his Southern roots but had a broader sense of life, unlike his relatives, who found it difficult to accept my mother because she was a Yankee interloper.

Or so I thought. I was forty years old when I learned the *real* story. Few things shock me, but this did. My mother had done something scandalous in her youth that raised eyebrows in Southern society. She had been married and divorced before she met my father, something that just wasn't done at the time. But when I heard the details, I thought this brief chapter in her life testified to her strength and independence.

When she was in her early twenties, Mother fell in love with a handsome and successful banker who was the life of the party. Their courtship played out at dances and picnics with friends, and he seemed like a solid and sociable beau who would make an ideal husband. Immediately after they married, however, he became a different person, a controlling man who tried to cut her off from the outside world. He went off to the bank every day while she was a prisoner in an ivory tower, left alone with a cook, a maid, and a driver who watched her every move and reported back to her possessive husband. She was not allowed to see her friends or visit her parents because he was insanely jealous.

Another woman might have resigned herself to the uncomfortable fate of a marriage that looked good because her husband seemed to be spoiling her but was fundamentally wrong. I'm sure many did, but not my mother. After four unhappy months, her husband committed the unpardonable sin of raising his voice to her, behavior she considered a warning sign and the last straw. She called her parents and told them to hurry over and pick her up. "And bring a truck," she said. She was not leaving the marriage empty-handed. In fact, immediately after she escaped from the house, she stopped at the furrier and bought four fur coats just to settle the score.

She got a divorce and set out to reclaim her life, which wasn't easy to do because a young woman who willfully walked away from a marriage in the 1930s was considered a hussy. From Big and Little Edie's point of view, a divorced Yankee was not a suitable bride for their brother. I'm sure they overcame their prejudices eventually because my mother was perfect.

As shocking as this revelation was to me, it underscored what I always knew about my parents. They were fiercely independent people who followed their own hearts and minds. My mother had the fortitude to walk away from a controlling man at a time when most women accepted that kind of situation as a life sentence. She and my father had chosen each other, and the past was nobody's business, although they decided it was more prudent to forget about that first marriage. It says a lot about how men and women were perceived that my father's reputation was never tainted by his thirty engagements, but my mother was defined by one failed marriage.

They married in 1938 at the Naval Academy in Annapolis, Maryland, and I was born in Jacksonville, Florida, where my father was modernizing a hospital, in 1941. I was named after my mother's half sister, Madelyn. My father picked my middle name, Patricia, because he imagined I would be petite and feminine, just like my mother, and he would call me Patsy. When I turned out to be a tomboy who towered over my mother, rode horses bareback, and played tennis, I decided that Patsy was too sweet and diminutive, so I changed it to Pat, although my parents always called me Madelyn.

My earliest memories are of our family being in constant motion, another way of saying we were vagabonds. My father often had high-level consulting jobs at hospitals all over the country, so, at various times, we lived in California, Texas, Florida, and Virginia, and my parents went to great lengths to make each place seem like home. There was always a selection of toys, a swing set (remember when they were made of metal and the poles lifted from the ground if you swung too vigorously? We're lucky we weren't all killed.), a bicycle, and pets—Fluffy, our enormous cat; Happy, my dog; and, later, Grey Ghost, my pony.

I loved Clearwater, Florida, where our house was right on the beach. The landscape in Florida was so different then—no high-rises, no thongs, no bottle service. Instead, long stretches of sand and the occasional quaint cottage hidden by tropical greenery. At our first house, our next-door neighbor was the writer John D. Mac-Donald, who was best known for his short stories in the 1940s and then went on to write bestselling crime thrillers, including the Travis McGee books. His son, Prentiss, was my best friend, and we spent idyllic days playing on the beach and in our gardens until a hurricane blew the roof off our house and we had to move to another.

I made friends wherever we lived, but my favorite playmate was my father. People often thought he was my grandfather because he was close to sixty and looked older than that, but he had the energy and enthusiasm of a much younger man. Lucky me, the fact that he was mostly retired meant that he had all the time in the world for me, and he had a great appetite for fun and adventure.

One of my favorite pastimes was listening to his stories as we turned the pages of the photo album that chronicled his world travels. The small black-and-white pictures showed sights most Americans had never seen—palaces, bamboo gardens, gorges, and rivers in China; villages in Nicaragua; his friend, Vajiravudh, one of the last kings of Siam. He described being on a gunboat and battling pirates on the Yangtze River, and he showed me pictures of his pet monkey, Joe, and his baby leopard. Father donated some of the exotic animals he adopted during his travels to the National Zoo in Washington, DC.

And, because he never treated me like a child, he allowed me to see the pictures in the back of the album—he had photographed the war victims who the Japanese slaughtered during the invasion of China, their fates documented for military records. Seventy-five years later, I'm still moved by the sight of the carnage.

My father even let me accompany him to the operating theaters in the hospitals he modernized. I sat there watching the operations, fascinated by procedures that might have scared other children. I was curious, and if my father thought I could handle the sight of surgeons at work, I knew I could.

We enjoyed more pastoral pastimes at our house in California, which was designed by my mother and bordered a vineyard. We spent time in the countryside, where he taught me how to fish and hunt, and I rode my horse—maybe a little too enthusiastically. I was only four years old when I fell off Grey Ghost and broke my hip. The treatment at the time was a cast that covered my lower body, making me look like a pint-size version of a mummy. I had to stay in bed for what seemed like forever, the worst kind of torture for an energetic child.

At one point, Father bought a helicopter, and we used it like the family car. It seemed perfectly normal to me to board the vibrating whirlybird and head off into the nearby mountains. One day, we flew to the church we attended on holidays, and I remember the other worshippers looking displeased when our landing disrupted the Easter service.

We often crisscrossed the country on "see the USA" road trips, which was my idea of hell because I would get carsick. Still, we were always game for new experiences and had a lot of fun along the way. Mother was the navigator, but she wasn't very good at reading maps, so we often got lost and ended up in strange places.

On one of our trips, Father may have gone a little too far when he made Mother try the sport of bowling at a place called Comanche Bowl, where they served Coca-Cola (which I wasn't allowed to drink because my mother thought it still contained cocaine—something she believed for the rest of her life). Picture petite Frances, who was always perfectly turned out in dresses—she never owned a pair of trousers—stockings, and high heels stepping up to the line to throw the heavy bowling ball. It's an unlikely image I'll never forget.

Mother didn't have much faith in the schools in Florida and California and wanted me to have a proper education, so, eventually, we settled in Richmond, Virginia, near her half sister, Madelyn, who lived in nearby Hopewell. We moved into a stately Georgian brick house, and she enrolled me in St. Catherine's, a fancy girl's school.

After I had been there a couple of weeks, she asked, "Well, what did you learn today?" When I told her I learned how to pour tea and curtsy, she said, "Oh my God, this is *not* what I consider an education." She quickly pulled me out of the school my mother thought was spending too much time on debutante preparation and enrolled me at Marymount, a Roman Catholic school that was ruled by French nuns who were academically oriented and *very* strict.

We studied Latin, French, math, geography—all the classics. The nuns expected us to work hard at our studies and conduct ourselves according to their elevated European standards. We had goûter, the French version of afternoon tea, every day promptly at four and conversed in French the entire time. We wore uniforms that were so shapeless it was hard to tell there were young women under all that fabric—but that was the point. We were there to cultivate our minds and our manners.

I was the only non-Catholic at the school, but I studied my Catechism diligently and won praise from my teachers for knowing my dogma inside out. I could recite the seven deadly sins like most children could name Snow White's seven dwarfs, so I learned something!

My education wasn't confined to school. My parents wanted me to share their appreciation for culture and the arts. When I was old enough, they took me on their trips abroad. In Europe, we visited museums and galleries, and my mother arranged for us to attend as many operas as humanely possible. Full disclosure: my father and I *never* shared her passion for opera. I wish I had asked her why she liked nothing more than listening to one diva or another sing—and, moreover, in another language—for hours at a time.

At home, my mother and I spent time at the Virginia Museum of Fine Arts, which had the largest collection of Fabergé eggs outside of Russia. I took art lessons and decorated my room with my drawings. I wasn't particularly talented, but I loved learning about artists and their art, an interest that began with our family visits to museums and galleries and stayed with me for the rest of my life.

Our home in Richmond reflected my parents' diverse tastes. While other houses in the city were filled with chintz, Williamsburg reproductions, and silver that had been buried during the Civil War, our decor was right out of *Auntie Mame*. Art deco rugs, Chinese vases, Eastern paintings, rare books, and collectibles from all over the world. My father displayed his vast collection of oriental objects on modern pieces, which my mother hated because she loved French furniture and pastel colors, but she always found a way to blend the disparate styles. The silver in our house was repoussé and Chinese and never spent a minute underground. I don't know how neighbors viewed our eclectic approach to design, but I thought we were sophisticated while they were slightly more provincial. We were Southern but with a kick and a twist.

Not Southern enough, however, to share the misguided belief held by my friends who thought that the White House in downtown Richmond, the former capital of the Confederacy, was the only one that counted (an idea handed down to them from their parents). I knew—and accepted—that the Union won the war and that the real White House and the real president were in Washington, DC.

And, thanks to my parents, I was taught that all people are equal, an outlier concept in the segregated South. My father greatly respected historical figures like Robert E. Lee *and* Abraham Lincoln. He took me to see both their birthplaces. I sat in Robert E. Lee's pew at our local Episcopal church and picnicked on the lawn at George Washington's Mount Vernon. Father had a wonderful way of making history come to life, and his understanding of the past was inclusive. We had to appreciate and honor what had come before us, but the same man who befriended the king of Siam and saved the lives of people of all colors and origins never viewed the world through the lens of racial prejudice. He and my mother fostered that same vision in me.

The prevailing attitude in Richmond was that household staff was "the help," and that was the tenor of life when I was growing up: domestic workers were paid next to nothing, undervalued, and often exploited. But the people who worked at our house were paid fair salaries and treated with respect: my parents were firm about that.

We were especially dependent on our cook because my mother, accomplished as she was, never mastered the domestic arts, meaning that she was clueless in the kitchen. The only recipe she knew how to make was a lime Jell-O mold with peaches and a square of cream cheese, no one's favorite dish. Mother managed the house beautifully, but she never cooked. And while my father enjoyed preparing Chinese food (a legacy from his travels), we couldn't live on his spicy (and sometimes unidentifiable) creations.

Our cook was a lovely woman. My father was so concerned about her comfort that he picked her up and drove her home every day, a small courtesy considering the magic she worked in the kitchen. I grew up on the best fried chicken (and fried chicken livers, which I still love today), collard greens, biscuits and gravy, and corn bread. Our cook was a single mother who was devoted to her son. When he was accepted at Howard University, my father paid his tuition because he believed everyone had a right to a good education.

While I was at Marymount, my parents heard about a coeducational Quaker boarding school in Ohio with a reputation for producing the highest number of Woodrow Wilson scholars in the country—the perfect place for me they decided. They were definitely motivated by their belief in the importance of a good education, but I think they were also concerned about something that had happened at Marymount.

One of the rites of passage at the school was a tea dance to celebrate the graduation of my eighth-grade class. It was supposed to be an innocent social gathering. Boys were imported from nearby private schools to dance with the girls, or we could invite a "little friend" to be our escort. Unbeknownst to my parents (until a concerned nun blew the whistle on me), *my* "little friend" was a handsome college student I met at our country club. He was more of a man than a boy—I think he was nineteen—and we had been dating for a few months. Let's just say I was more physically developed than most girls my age.

My parents wanted to see the last of him (and I was ready to move on), so off I went to Ohio. I was excited about my new school, and the first thing that struck me was the diverse student body. We were our own little United Nations, with students from Spain, Japan, Korea, Canada, and other countries, and two Black students, so it was a very different experience for someone who had been in school in the segregated South. In fact, some of my classmates were freedom fighters who had traveled to Mississippi to protest segregation. One of the Black students—we were good friends who played basketball in the gym all the time—went on to become "Mr. World," an international bodybuilding champion, which may have seemed an unusual career choice for a potential Woodrow Wilson scholar.

The academic program was rigorous, and the school also taught us the importance of public service. We had to be mindful of the community and participate in charitable activities on weekends—that was the Quaker way. We attended a Quaker meeting every Thursday and Sunday, a time to sit and reflect. Learning how to meditate at a young age made it easy for me to do it later in life.

Lest I paint too saintly a portrait of my high school years, let me add that we knew how to have a good time and did so whenever possible. Boys and girls could go skating (and hold hands!), take walks, and attend socials. The golden ticket was a permission slip. If a parent signed a slip, a student could go to another student's home for the weekend, and then all rules were off, meaning that we might slip into a dance at a local high school and learn the steps to the hot new dance, the bop.

When I was a freshman, my beau was a senior named Warren. He came from a wealthy family in Illinois that owned an aviation business and had a convertible and a plane. Despite my parents' concern about my brief May/December relationship when I was at Marymount, they really did trust me implicitly, so they allowed me to fly home with him for weekend visits, with Warren piloting the plane. We stayed with his mother and would do things like go to a state fair and ride the Ferris wheel.

(Let me be clear: I would never allow a child of mine to fly on a plane piloted by a teenager.)

The entire time I was in high school, nobody did drugs, nobody smoked, and, blessedly, nobody got knocked up. There were three categories of sex way back then: necking, petting, and going all the way. We didn't know much about anatomy and thought if you dared to go all the way, you automatically got pregnant, so we respected the guardrails and were relatively chaste. For the most part, we were a pretty tame group.

But that's how it was in the 1950s, relaxed, fun, and safe, like *Happy Days*, *Leave It to Beaver*, and *Father Knows Best*. In Richmond, we ate at tearooms and walked to places at night. When I was sixteen or seventeen, my parents let me get a black party dress at Montaldo's, a very fancy dress shop. I felt like the most sophisticated person in the world, but, of course, I wore it with Mary Janes, pearls, and little white gloves, so I didn't look like the siren I imagined. I always say that we were lucky to come of age in this sleepy time because we weren't bored by innocent pleasures. Without the Internet, social media, TikTok, and all the other Pandora's boxes that opened in the ensuing years, we couldn't even imagine the temptations ahead.

Recently, I was going through some old photographs and suddenly remembered all the accidents I had at boarding school—when broken bones were a way of life. During my first week in Ohio, a boy squirted me with a water gun, and I chased him down the hall to retaliate. Just as I caught up with him, he slammed a heavy oak door with Tiffany glass panels, and my elbow went through the glass. The wound was so deep and jagged that it looked as if I had been attacked by a shark. My poor father had to fly to Ohio to oversee my stitches.

Another time, my friend Vicky and I snuck over to a neighboring farm to go horseback riding. I loved horses and was an experienced rider, but snow was on the ground, and the horse we borrowed stepped into a hole while we were galloping. Vicky was sitting behind me and holding on to my waist, so I was unable to do an emergency dismount when the horse tried to throw me off, and I fell under him. Then he jumped over me and broke my sternum. My father had to come back for that accident, too.

And a year later, the same horse stepped on my foot and broke two bones, prompting another emergency visit from my father. He may have regretted sending me to Ohio.

I was on my own when I had an unusual accident at a riding camp in Ireland. Most summers, I went to a riding camp in the Blue Ridge Mountains, where we rode English style on thoroughbreds. I was becoming a serious equestrian and needed to train at a proper stable, so my parents sent me to a fancy riding school in Ireland. The horses were big—they measured sixteen hands—and one day, the instructors had us jump over low stone walls. I fell off and landed on a piece of barbed wire. The Irish doctor who took care of the wound on my derriere must have had a sense of humor because he stitched it in the shape of an *X*. When it healed, I had a white scar that looked like a big kiss. The funny thing is that *none* of my husbands noticed it. But whenever I see it, I feel like a centerfold. Ah, the mishaps of my youth.

Like my father, I was somewhat of a dichotomy because while I received a top-notch liberal education from the Quakers in Ohio, I also prepared for one of the most retro Southern traditions, my official debut into Richmond society. Second only to a wedding in important social rituals, the debut involved wearing a virginal white dress and being presented to the elite members of the community.

Grandmother Mandy, my mother's mother, wanted to do something special for me on this big occasion. I had very thick, unruly hair, and a new process called a "permanent wave" promised to turn even the most rebellious locks into smooth curls. My hair was uncontrollable and could benefit from taming. My grandmother made the arrangements, and I reported to the beauty salon for my big treatment. The hairdresser sectioned my hair and wrapped it around what looked like chicken bones. Then, she applied a foul-smelling formula that was so strong (and, now that I think about it, probably so *toxic*) that it made my eyes tear.

It did more than that. When the "bones" were removed, I was left with hair that looked like the Bride of Frankenstein had stuck her finger—maybe her whole hand—in an electrical outlet. My short hair stood out from my head in evil twists: Medusa on steroids. I started crying uncontrollably, and this time my tears were real.

There was absolutely nothing we could do about it. The only solution was to wait for the hair to grow out and then cut it. But time was not my friend. The debutante ball was imminent, so I had no choice but to show this unfortunate hairstyle to the world.

On the night of the ball, I put on my beautiful white dress with the pink bow in the back, descended the stairs at the Jefferson

Hotel, and danced the first dance with my father. We were assigned escorts from the local military academy for the dances that followed. The evening is a blur, but I do remember feeling humiliated when my friends laughed at my hair—they thought it was hysterical. I thought it was a tragedy.

Needless to say, there's not a single photograph from that terrible evening, and I wouldn't have it any other way.

Two

———— • ————

While I was still at boarding school, my parents moved from our house to an apartment in Richmond because my father's health was deteriorating. He had been diagnosed with leukemia and was having trouble navigating the stairs. Then, in 1959, immediately after my eighteenth birthday, he passed away and was buried at Arlington National Cemetery. He was seventy-seven, which seemed so old at the time. Now, I think of it as middle age. Unlike most men in the 1940s and 1950s, my father was so present in my life that his absence left a huge void. My mother and I were devastated—lost—and the only way we could imagine moving forward was to keep moving. We planned a whirlwind tour of Europe, hoping that traveling from one destination to another would distract us from our terrible loss.

My mother had another motivation for spiriting me out of the country. During my senior year, I had a star-crossed relationship with a sophomore at Dartmouth who came from a wealthy Jewish family. His parents disapproved of me because I wasn't Jewish, and my mother disapproved of *him* because his family had the nerve to consider me inappropriate. She hoped traveling would put an out-of-sight, out-of-mind end to this Romeo-and-Juliet dilemma.

The trip established a pattern that would continue for years to come. My mother and I, along with many suitcases, set off to see the world together. I wasn't allowed to wear blue jeans on our first trip, so packing was more complicated because I had to have dresses and skirts—and their accessories—for all occasions. We traveled to Europe on the RMS *Queen Mary*, praised as the most elegant and sophisticated luxury liner when it launched in 1936. The ship was still impressive, and even though some people preferred to fly transcontinental, I appreciated a leisurely ocean crossing.

We stayed in France for a few months, planned our next destinations, and settled into a routine. I visited museums and galleries, and my mother went to every major opera house with me in tow. One activity we could always agree on was shopping. We cut a wide swath through the boutiques in Paris. Moving along, we floated down the Rhine on some kind of flatboat, celebrated Oktoberfest in a raucous beer garden, and, in Vienna, tasted the original Sacher torte at the Hotel Sacher and watched the famous Lipizzan horses dance.

Of course we went to the Vienna State Opera. I like listening to the Three Tenors when they sing classical favorites, and I did have the privilege of hearing Luciano Pavarotti, Plácido Domingo, and José Carreras at their legendary concert at the Baths of Caracalla in Rome in 1990, but that's about my limit. On this trip, I spent hours, maybe years, listening to sopranos serenade tenors.

My most thrilling evening at the opera happened in Vienna. I can't recall the opera's name or who the soprano was that night, but I remember the stage had a long banquet table set with candelabras. The diva was singing to a man wearing a cape when she moved a little too close to the candle, and her wig caught on fire. She didn't realize what was happening and was shocked when the man, who was standing directly behind her so she couldn't see him, pulled off his cape and started beating her with it to extinguish the flames. He took care of the situation so quickly that she was never in any real danger, but I, along with the rest of the audience, watched breathlessly because I'd never seen anything so exciting at an opera—and probably never will again.

Our agenda was rigorous. But what did I do for fun? I was a teenager, after all, and culture (and shopping, lots of shopping) can only take a girl so far. My mother would go to bed at eight o'clock every night, and I didn't. Not that I snuck out and went crazy. My gentlemen callers always asked my mother for permission to take me out on a date, so it was all very proper. I remember flirtations with a boat captain, a handsome maître d' at our hotel, and a New Zealander who loved to dance.

Mother and I took many trips together, and she was a fearless traveler, curious about everything. Sometimes, she was too daring. When we were in Australia, she wanted to see Uluru, formerly called Ayers Rock. The sacred red monolith, home to the Pitjantjatjara people, was very hard to get to, so Mother hired the only available transportation, a Fokker World War II airplane. Well, they *called* it an airplane, but it looked more like something a child might put together with a model kit. When we arrived at the "airport," a technician—who was really just a guy with a screwdriver—had to set up scaffolding, prop up the wings, and screw in bolts to keep them in place.

Our confidence had nowhere to go but up until the pilot reported for duty. He was accompanied by a barely dressed young woman (*his copilot, perhaps?*) who climbed into the plane and sat on his lap. They closed the curtain to the aptly named cockpit and lifted off, giving new meaning to the line "Fasten your seat belts, this is going to be a bumpy ride." I don't know what Mother was thinking, but I wondered if this was a new twist on the Mile High Club.

We landed, and the pilot and his friend emerged from their love nest wearing safari hats draped with thick nets. We had no such protection, so when we disembarked, we were devoured by swarming flies. It was 120 degrees, and we were not happy. That's my memory of Uluru.

On another New Zealand flight, we flew through a pass so narrow that the wings came *this* close to the mountains on either side. I didn't think we would make it. We also went to Nome, Alaska, because Mother had it in her head that she wanted to see Russia. It was there—somewhere in the distance—but, not surprisingly, she couldn't see it.

Our funniest travel misadventure happened in New Guinea when Mother decided she wanted to tour local places that might be interesting. The concierge at our hotel called a taxi and told the driver where to take us. We had no idea where we were going and ended up in Goroka, a remote village nestled in the highlands of Papua. Goroka was home to the Asaro Mudmen, who performed ritual dances to ward off enemies.

When the Mudmen appeared, their bodies were covered with chalky white mud, and their faces were obscured with grimacing oversize masks. What was *not* obscured were their muddy dingdongs, which dipped and swayed as they moved. The age-old ritual was impressive, but it was hard to look anywhere else when we saw this unexpected display.

When we returned to the hotel, the concierge was shocked to hear that we had seen the Mudmen—that's *not* where he instructed the taxi driver to take us. "They're cannibals," he told us. Well, we lived to tell the tale, so we must not have been juicy enough to be on the menu.

Travels with my mother were never boring.

The real or imagined threat of the Mudmen paled compared to a near-death experience I had in Tahiti. We went there in search of Gauguin, one of my favorite artists. I wanted to see the tropical landscapes that inspired his paintings and visit the Gauguin Museum. We hired a car and driver to tour the island—you can drive the entire perimeter of Tahiti in a day—and set off to see the sights.

The museum was disappointing because the only "art" on view turned out to be large black-and-white reproductions of Gauguin paintings. But the island itself was magical. We stopped at a restaurant on the beach. The view was extraordinary: a lagoon with a floating dock stretching out over the water. I grabbed my fancy Leica camera and walked out onto the dock. The camera was new, and I really didn't know how to use it, so I sat down, took off my espadrilles, and dangled my feet in the water while I attempted to figure out the light meter.

Suddenly, the placid waters started swirling, and out of the corner of my eye, I saw men on the shore running in my direction, shouting something in French. When the deck lurched, I knew I was in trouble. Holding on for dear life, I looked at the water and saw a chain-link fence under the surface with sharks thrashing inside. I was sitting atop a shark pen, dangling my legs like tasty bait. I got up on my hands and knees and crawled to safety. One more second and I would have been yanked into the pen by the hungry sharks. This was not the tranquil Gauguin experience I'd imagined.

I escaped another watery grave in Australia when I went snorkeling off Green Island in the Great Barrier Reef. I rented my equipment at a little shack and swam out to see the incredible fish and coral reefs. On my way back to shore, I noticed a group of Japanese tourists who were wearing white plastic boots. Curious, I asked the attendant at the shack why they were dressed that way.

"They don't want to step on a stonefish," he said matter-of-factly. "It sits in the sand, and if you step on it, you die."

I looked at my bare feet and thought about the timing of his warning. "Well, just as an item of curiosity," I said to him, "shouldn't you suggest boots to people *before* they go into the water? Maybe put up a *big* sign?"

Mishaps aside, I enjoyed every trip with my mother. When I look back on these adventures, I also feel closer to my father. My memories are like those fading snapshots in the album that chronicled his storied life. Seeing the world opened his mind and heart to new people, places, and ideas, and I'd like to think I've benefited in the same way.

Our first European tour lasted about a year, and then it was time for me to start classes at George Washington University. I loved Richmond, but I knew that Washington, DC, would be a more exciting place to live, and I was starting to think about my future. My mother, a trailblazer when she became a highly trained army nurse in the 1930s, gave me great advice. "Make a career, not a job," she said. "A job is temporary, but a career is something you can always fall back on." My primary interests were art and art history. I took my coursework very seriously and always looked for opportunities to take advantage of the extraordinary resources in DC—especially the Smithsonian and the National Gallery.

My personal life took an unexpected turn when I went on a date and met someone else's date, a young man named Lon Smith. Lon was only twenty-five, but he was already the head of Dun & Bradstreet in Washington, overseeing a staff of fifty people. At night, he was studying for his MBA at American University. He was smart, ambitious, successful, and appealing. He called me for a date, and we moved rapidly from *like* to *love* to *let's get married*.

Why the rush? It's a Southern thing that women need to be married by the time they're twenty-five or they automatically become old maids. I still had a few years before my expiration date, but I've always been a risk-taker. I couldn't imagine having a better husband than Lon. And if I were wrong about that, I thought, *Well, there's always divorce.*

Three

When I told my mother about our engagement, she asked, "Do you want a big wedding, or do you want the money?"

I said, "I want the money!" There was no hesitation at all. I was never the girl who fantasized about her wedding day, and I'd been a bridesmaid enough times to know that weddings were a big waste of money and an emotional minefield.

My Southern girlfriends made albums where they pasted pictures of floral arrangements, cakes, wedding dresses, veils, bridesmaid dresses, headgear for the attendants, and even houses with white picket fences, their happily-ever-after destinations. The only thing missing was the groom, but he seemed to matter the least in these fantasies. I thought it was all ridiculous.

The wedding-day feuds I witnessed were even crazier. One of my friends married a man with very difficult parents. The bride arranged for the florist to place a pretty bouquet with ribbons by her mother's seat, a sweet gesture. The groom's mother spotted the bouquet, *saw red*, and snatched the flowers off the pew, leading to an altercation in the aisle. Not the best way to kick off a wedding.

Considering the possibility of moments like this, ugly brides-maid dresses, mediocre food, and hours spent with relatives I barely knew, not to mention the groom's relatives, whom I would never see again, I chose to get married by a minister in an intimate ceremony with no pageantry. I wore a short peach dress and a hat with a veil. Lon was thrilled because it was all so easy.

We moved in together without missing a beat in our busy sched-ules. I may have been an unusual newlywed. I had my own ideas about sleeping arrangements. I'm not prudish about intimacy, but like many Europeans, I always insisted on having separate bedrooms and bathrooms. People would be happier if they did that—they'd get more sleep because bed partners frequently snore and pull at the covers. And sleeping in separate bedrooms is *very* romantic, like something in a Regency novel. Are you going to his room? Is he coming to yours? Or are you both tired and just going to sleep? Not that I ever slept alone. I always had—and still have—a dog or a cat in my bed.

Like my mother before me, I never learned how to cook, so I was an eager and early adopter when Swanson launched an enhanced TV dinner, complete with dessert. However, I failed to read the instruc-tions and didn't realize that the little tray had to be taken out of the box before it was heated, so after I bungled even the preparation of a TV dinner, we pivoted to meals at the local Howard Johnson's.

I did have a sense that I would be very good at entertaining, although my first attempt was such a disaster that it is best forgotten. Unfortunately, for those who witnessed the debacle, the evening lives in infamy. Lon and I invited a few friends to come over for dinner on a Saturday night. Let's start with the menu. Someone had given me a book called *You Can Cook If You Can Read*, which I think was the 1960s equivalent of *Cooking for Dummies*. I was secure about my reading skills, so I selected a recipe for beef stroganoff. Instead of serving our guests wine, we plied them with a lethal mixture of bourbon and Coke.

My glass was never empty as I threw together the ingredients. Subsequently, I got to the point where I *couldn't* read and started improvising. The stroganoff curdled into a mess that one of my guests described politely as monkey barf. The noodles stuck together like petrified worms. And someone screamed (was it me?) when a dish towel caught fire. No lives were lost, but by this point, I had misplaced all my inhibitions. The only sane response to this series of disasters, I decided, was to take off my clothes and go to bed.

I remember hearing faint goodbyes from my unfortunate guests as they rushed to the exit (and probably the nearest pizza parlor). The next day, I pulled myself together and imposed a sentence of watching Julia Child until I better understood what goes into a successful meal . . . even if I would never cook it myself. My key takeaway from my failed attempt to be a hostess was always to call a caterer.

I was far more skilled at school, especially in my art history and archaeology classes, and in 1963, I was rewarded with a fellowship at the Smithsonian. I reported to the History and Technology building to work under the direction of Dr. Richard Howland, an eminence in the fields of classical archaeology and art history and preservation. My assignments included helping conservators with the First Ladies' gowns and the presidential silver and dinnerware, and on one occasion, I slowly and *very* carefully cleaned a delicate ostrich carousel figure from the Van Alstyne Folk Art exhibit. It was incredible for a junior in college to have access to these treasures, and the experience confirmed my ambition to pursue a master's degree in art history and archaeology after I graduated from college.

Dr. Howland introduced me to another fascinating mentor and friend—Clement Conger. Clem was dubbed "the Grand Acquisitor" because when he served as chairman of the Fine Arts Committee and curator of the Diplomatic Reception Rooms for the State Department, he successfully appealed to private donors to fund donations of antique furniture, paintings, porcelain, and silver, transforming the dreary State reception rooms into showcases of American treasures. One writer quipped that Clem "raised more money for the United States government than anyone outside the Internal Revenue Service."

We had a lot in common—he was from Virginia—and we shared a love of the decorative arts. I always enjoyed our conversations because I had so much to learn from him. But one afternoon, when we were on the phone, he ended the call abruptly. He was working at the White House that day and had just gotten word that the president had been shot. November 22, 1963. Everyone who lived through JFK's assassination has never forgotten where they were and what they were doing when they heard the news.

Lon and I were glued to the television for days, seeing one shocking image after another, including Jack Ruby shooting Lee Harvey Oswald in real time on our screen. I remember how sad I felt when we watched the coverage of JFK's funeral. It was estimated that a million people lined the streets to pay tribute to the president on that cold day, yet Washington was eerily silent. The impact of the assassination was so great that we all struggled to think of anything else.

About a year later, my friend Susan and I decided to treat ourselves to an early dinner at the Jockey Club, a very fancy place in Washington. We were unfashionably early, so the dining room was empty, or so I thought.

As we got up to leave, Susan whispered to me, "I can't believe they're here!"

Who? I didn't notice anyone until I saw a couple in the corner.

"That's Jackie Kennedy and Marlon Brando," she said excitedly.

In a way, I'm glad I didn't know they were there because I doubt that I would have been able to stop staring.

We left them to their tête-à-tête, exited the restaurant, and tucked away the memory. How many people know that the former First Lady had a long, secretive lunch with Marlon Brando?

I've been asked if people in academia took me seriously, considering that I was young, Southern, and a *woman* in the not-so-enlightened early sixties. I wrote my thesis (a treatise on the origins of Helios, the sun king, that required me to comb through Sanskrit manuscripts and other equally obscure source material) and completed my coursework in one year, so I was definitely serious. Yet, I'll never forget the time a friend, bless her heart, introduced me to someone and said, "She's not as dumb as she looks or sounds"—all because I was a reasonably attractive woman with a Southern accent, which I guess was doubly negative.

No one doubted my skills when I went to Ostia, near Pompeii and Herculaneum, on my first archaeological dig, although my role there was not what I imagined. I thought I'd be Howard Carter, uncovering lost treasure. Instead, I was Annie Oakley, sharpshooter. When my professors discovered that I knew how to use a gun (courtesy of my father's hunting lessons), that talent trumped my academic credentials, and I was armed, positioned outside the tomb, and asked to shoot any snakes that might try to get inside while my colleagues were studying marriage sarcophagi. I never found—or even got close to—a single artifact, but I killed at least twenty vipers.

While I was a graduate student, the university offered me a job as an instructor. I taught Introductory Art and the History of Western Civilization, a two-semester survey course. My students were just a couple of years younger than me, but we were worlds apart. Dressed in sheaths and little heels or my knockoff Oleg Cassini boots—my hair teased into a perky bouffant—I channeled

Jacqueline Kennedy, the country's fashion icon. On the other side of the lectern were 150 kids who fell into identifiable groups: the sassy fraternity boys; the football players who loved the class because I turned off the lights when I showed slides, and they could sleep; and the Age of Aquarius flower children, who smoked marijuana in the bathroom, staged sit-ins in the president's office, and didn't seem to own any shoes.

The frat boys were the most entertaining (the jocks dozed, and the would-be hippies were in a mellow world of their own). They knew I was married, but that didn't stop them from trying to flirt with me after class. One bold student wrote a message on the enormous blackboard at the front of the classroom. "My teacher is soft as bunny fur / I think I'd like to sleep with her." *At least he knows how to rhyme*, I thought.

When I showed slides of Chartres Cathedral and other medieval buildings and asked my students to identify the supporting structure, some wise guy would call out "flying buttocks" instead of buttress, typical frat boy humor.

Funny moments aside, those of us who taught at the time shouldered a heavy responsibility. Our students had to get passing grades in our classes because if they failed and flunked out of school, they would be drafted into the military and sent to Vietnam. When I looked at the students who could barely manage a D, I felt compassion and wanted to help. I assigned them special projects and worked with them after class until I was certain they could pass the course.

Eventually, I became an assistant professor at GW. When I look back, I'm very proud of the three programs I established for the School of Continuing Education at the university. It was difficult for housewives—now we call them stay-at-home moms—to attend college because most classes ran for one hour and were scheduled multiple times a week. I set up an art history class that met for three hours once a week, a much more manageable way for the women to get their course credit.

I also launched an evening class for veterans—many fresh from Vietnam—who worked during the day and were trying to get their degrees at night. They were such good students, focused and dedicated, and it never would have occurred to them to sleep through a class. They were there to do the work. Even though I had to drive from Virginia to the Veterans Administration Building in downtown Washington in the dark of night and haul my projector and slides into a deserted office building, it was worth it to help these young men realize their ambitions.

The third program may have been the most ambitious of all. I took fifteen students on a three-week tour of the capitals of Europe to study art, sculpture, painting, and architecture. If it sounds like the opening of a sitcom or a reality show, it was. Lon, who was such a good sport, was my co-chaperone. Our misadventures began when we arrived in London, our first destination, and discovered that the travel agent, who had collected all our money in advance, had neglected to pay the hotel. Our American Express card, which had never seen so much action, footed the charges for the entire group. We knew the university would reimburse us, but it was an inauspicious start.

Chaperoning fifteen teenagers (before cell phones were invented) was daunting—it was like herding cats. I realized fairly quickly that no young person had come to Europe to behave. And they didn't see me as an authority figure because I was only about eight years older than most of them. Right after we arrived in Italy, a student who must have been more sophisticated than she looked disappeared for a few days when she ran off with a cute crew member from our Alitalia flight who was staying at our hotel. Our truant took one look at him and decided it was time for a little Roman holiday. The fact that she was the daughter of the president of an Ivy League university raised the stakes *and* my anxiety level. I practically held my breath until she returned—just as we were leaving for Spain.

Another student came home after curfew and was locked out of the hotel. Most of the kids didn't know how to get up in the morning or pack a suitcase, but they were very good at complaining. Lon and I began to question why *anyone* would ever have children.

I have one happy memory from the trip. While we were in Rome, we toured the catacombs, and as we boarded our tour bus to return to the hotel, a man asked if he could have a ride back to the city. Lon and I had plenty of room and welcomed the chance to speak to an adult. He was so appreciative that he offered the two of us a private tour of the Vatican and the pope's apartment. I know that sounds suspicious, but the gentleman turned out to be one of the pope's secretaries.

Lon and I arranged to meet him the next night (our students were on lockdown in the hotel) and had the experience of a lifetime. As promised, our new friend walked us through the Sistine Chapel, then took us to the pope's private apartment—His Holiness was away at his summer house. The rooms were filled with art that no one ever sees: works by Rembrandt, Leonardo, and other great artists. I felt incredibly privileged and grateful, and the magic of this extraordinary tour almost (but not quite) compensated for the nightmare of chaperoning our rambunctious charges.

Usually, I'm sad when I board the plane home from Europe. Not *this* time.

Ask Me Anything:

Dating and Relationships

I'm confused. Is it appropriate to flirt in 2025?

I think flirting is always appropriate because I define it as giving someone all your attention and presenting your best, high-wattage self. Smile, laugh, use your eyes and hands expressively, and be the person who can talk to anyone about anything. Being attentive is a sign of good manners, and if we're talking about a potentially romantic situation, you can be playful and engaged without being sexual. Southerners are very good at this.

I'm tired of swiping on dating apps. How can I meet a real person, or does that not happen anymore?

It can happen if you're more proactive. There's nothing wrong with telling friends you're interested in meeting someone and asking if they know anyone who might be a good match. There are ways of spending one's time that put you in the vicinity of eligible partners, such as joining museum groups. My mother always told me that even if I knew the person who asked me out wasn't Mr. Right, I should go out and mingle because I might meet someone else. She

was right. I met two of my husbands at events I attended with someone else. Oh, and if you're a woman, stop going out with a bevy of
girlfriends. By traveling in a pack, you're limiting your opportunities
to meet people. One final thought—don't go to tacky places. You're
never going to meet Prince Charming in a dive bar.

How can I make a good impression on a first date?
Don't talk about past romantic relationships, don't flaunt or expose
your physical attributes, don't share your myriad food restrictions,
and never order spinach because it will end up stuck between your
teeth. I think a little mystery on a first date goes a long way.

Four

❧⚭❨

I may have equated the trip abroad as an existential form of birth control, but a couple of months after we got home, at the age of twenty-eight, I discovered I was pregnant. It was good news. Lon and I had reached the point in our marriage when we felt ready to have a child. We had a lovely house in a gated community in the Washington suburbs, so there was plenty of room for a baby. My mother and Lon's mother lived nearby and were eager to report for duty as grandmothers. And I had a flexible schedule at the university and knew my job would be waiting for me whenever I wanted to return to work.

I continued teaching until I was about eight months pregnant, and I had to wear clothes that made me look like a beach cabana. The designers who created maternity clothes in the sixties were sadists. The dresses were ugly and shapeless, and they usually attempted to hide the baby under infantilizing bows, as if these innocent decorations could make people forget that sex started the whole process. The dresses that tried to be more modern were just silly. I had one with a bull's-eye stamped directly over my protruding abdomen, in case the baby's location wasn't obvious.

Today, the pendulum has swung in the other direction, and we "celebrate the bump." I'm glad that pregnant women no longer dress like oversize toddlers, but I would love to tell the expectant mother who proudly squeezes herself into a Hervé Léger bandage dress in her tenth month that I would prefer *not* to see the baby kicking like a Rockette.

I was enormous in the final days of my pregnancy, which should have been foreshadowing. Whitney Sudler-Smith entered the world on June 2, 1968, as the new heavyweight champion—a whopping ten pounds. He was so big and screamed so loudly that the hospital staff had to isolate him from the other newborns because they thought he might scare them. Fortunately, he was beautiful, with perfectly formed features, and once he stopped crying, he had the sweetest disposition.

After his dramatic entrance, Whitney was an easy baby. Soon after we brought him home from the hospital, we temporarily moved to New York City while Lon, who was becoming a stockbroker, attended a four-month business seminar on Wall Street. I got all the exercise I needed pushing the carriage around the Upper East Side and lifting Whitney, who was huge, a hundred times a day. It was better than any boot camp. By the time we returned to Washington, I was lean (the thinnest I've ever been, in fact) and strong.

I viewed motherhood as another subject to master and did lots of research, relying on experts like Dr. Benjamin Spock to help me navigate this unfamiliar terrain. Of course I made mistakes. Any mother who has dressed her infant in a cute-as-a-button starched outfit learns that projectile vomiting will inevitably soon follow.

When I felt more confident, I relied on my instincts, raising Whitney the way I had been raised by my parents. I wanted him to be imaginative and curious, but I also stressed the importance of good manners. Lon was my partner in this mission, and Whitney was lucky to have his wonderful father as a role model. Lon was the perfect gentleman. He stood when I entered the room and opened my car door. So many of these niceties have disappeared because they're viewed as old-fashioned or anti-feminist, but I think that civility and respect for others are never out of place.

We settled into a routine for the next few years. We moved to Virginia, and I resumed teaching but maintained a light schedule until Whitney started nursery school. My time with my son was precious. Lon and I were only children and planned on having one child, so Whitney was everything. As promised, his grandmothers couldn't get enough of their grandson and were always ready for babysitting opportunities.

Whitney himself might have something to say about being the focus of so much attention, but I think he thrived. He was whip-smart even as a child, and Lon predicted that he would follow in his footsteps and have a future in finance. But Whitney was creative and more interested in the arts—reading, writing, drawing, and music—so we sent him to Georgetown Day School, where we knew he would get a good liberal education.

We also took him on trips. We went to London when he was about five and stayed at The Dorchester—a beautiful hotel known for its high level of service. Whitney was fascinated by the doormen, who dressed in uniforms and wore white gloves—so fascinated that he decided his aim in life was to become a doorman. When we got home, my mother gave him a pair of old white gloves, and he manned our front door, imitating the moves he saw at The Dorchester. At some point, he outgrew that ambition, although, like his mother, he always had an affinity for everything British.

And then there was the time I tried to raise his consciousness. Whitney collected G.I. Joe figures, and when he got together with his young friends, mostly boys around the same age, they played war. Being a feminist, I decided to buy Whitney the new Dr. Barbie doll that came out in 1973, when the women's liberation movement was in full swing. She was a trailblazer, dressed in scrubs and a lab coat and equipped with a stethoscope. I thought she'd be a welcome addition to the war zone because she could treat the wounded, but none of the boys seemed terribly excited to have Dr. Barbie on call.

After about an hour, I heard hooting and hollering and thought they might have had a change of heart, so I went downstairs to see how Dr. Barbie was doing. The poor doll had been stripped and cast into a tent while G.I. Joe was wearing her lab coat and treating patients. My feminist fantasy wasn't meant to be.

After we moved to our new house in Virginia, Lon started entertaining clients at home, and this was when I developed my style as a hostess. There was no way in hell I would repeat the beef stroganoff disaster I experienced as a newlywed—it was better for me (and our guests) if I kept my distance from the stove and any sharp objects. I saw myself as more of an impresario who has good ideas and knows how to bring them to life. A dinner party is a form of theater; with the right setting, props, and food sleight of hand, an ordinary meal can be extraordinary.

One evening, I ordered Chinese food from our local restaurant and placed the white cardboard containers in antique silver tureens. Our guests feasted on a banquet of takeout paired with fine wines (courtesy of Lon, who had become a wine expert). No one can be *too* serious while stuffing moo shu pork into pancakes or eating fried rice with chopsticks, so everyone relaxed and had fun. On another occasion, I did the same thing with Mexican food, and the evening turned into a fiesta.

The showstopper—and everyone's favorite—was the traditional fried chicken dinner prepared by our housekeeper. There wasn't a socialite or a financier on the planet who could resist her Southern comfort food, and it was amusing to watch people who were usually very buttoned-up tearing into a crispy chicken leg or slathering butter on a piece of corn bread. We're all children at a picnic when there's fried chicken on the table. I provided finger bowls to erase all evidence of the debauchery.

I learned that the secret to being a good hostess is not to be boring. Guests love the unexpected—a whimsical menu, unusual table decorations (I've used everything from custom-made cookies serving as place cards to plastic alligators demonstrating positions from the Kama Sutra—to be clear, this risqué grouping was for a stag dinner). Entertaining can be as much fun for the hostess as it's supposed to be for the guests if the party is playful instead of pretentious.

And it's never about money. Excess never impresses me. I've been to events that burned through staggering budgets to re-create Versailles's Hall of Mirrors, but the effect was "Am I dead yet?"

Sometimes a party can be *too* lively. We discovered that when we adopted Jaws, an adorable basset hound. We named him after we saw Steven Spielberg's blockbuster movie because our puppy had so much in common with the titular shark. He ate *everything*, including a Smithfield ham he yanked from a serving table during a party. Somehow, he managed to growl and chew simultaneously, so no one was brave enough to take it away from him. That was the evening's entertainment.

One of our houseguests was not amused when Jaws broke into her bedroom, ransacked her suitcase, and swallowed her diaphragm. But that wasn't the worst part. Jaws ran downstairs to the cocktail party I was hosting for a famous senator and, coincidentally but with a great homing instinct, coughed up the diaphragm at the embarrassed owner's feet. No one knew where to look. I quickly whisked it away, knowing the incident would live in legend. I'm still talking about it today.

Nor was I amused when Jaws crashed a party I hosted for a friend who was launching a high-end jewelry line. We had set up a display of her best pieces for the guests to shop, but somehow Jaws got there first, opened all the leather pouches, and absconded with a valuable sapphire-and-diamond ring, which he swallowed. The vet gave me the bad news that the only course of action was to feed him a shocking amount of Wonder bread and wait for the ring to work its way through his system. Three days later, the ring appeared. Jaws was fine, but the ring needed an industrial cleaning.

I was Perle Mesta at night and a carpool mom during the day. When Whitney was in kindergarten, I became friendly with Alan and Kate Novak, the parents of his best friend. Sometimes these relationships are all about arranging playdates, but I was delighted to find out that Alan's sister was Barbara Novak, the greatest living art historian. Barbara was the chairman of the Art History department at Barnard College and was revered for her seminal book *American Painting of the Nineteenth Century: Realism, Idealism, and the American Experience*, which I used when I taught my classes. We met and bonded over our shared passion for nineteenth-century American art.

Then Alan, who was a successful businessman and owned several companies, introduced us to an extremely wealthy art lover in his circle, someone who would be considered a billionaire today. The gentleman had an unusual ambition *and* a plan. He wanted to build the finest collection of American art that money could buy, and he proposed that Barbara and I help him. He said that he would underwrite the endeavor, emphasizing that money was no object. His one caveat was that he had to remain anonymous: we were not allowed to reveal his identity to anyone . . . ever.

If it sounds like a fairy tale, in a way it was. Thanks to our generous benefactor, the job of art adviser came with the best imaginable perks—unlimited resources for buying the greatest art available, first-class travel, and the finest hotels. Barbara and I were empowered to travel the country—if necessary, the world—in search of the best of the best examples of American art, and we had separate roles. It was my job to find the paintings, which meant visiting galleries, auction houses, and private collections. When I did track down a prospective acquisition, Barbara, the world-renowned scholar, assessed the work, reviewed the provenance, and, if everything passed her tough standards, authenticated it. She never got involved with the finances because that would have been a conflict of interest.

Working as an art adviser seemed like the job I was always meant to do. The thrill of the chase was exhilarating, and it was a good—no, the *best*—time to focus on nineteenth-century American art. The bicentennial in 1976 sparked a new wave of patriotism, and people were interested in all things American, including artists from the previous century. Their works could be anywhere—on a great-aunt's living room wall, where a painting had hung for decades, or tucked away in an attic because it was too old-fashioned for contemporary taste. Wonderful discoveries could be made, prices established, and long-forgotten stories told. In a way, searching for these paintings was a form of archaeology, but this time, I didn't have to shoot any vipers.

I gave up teaching and immersed myself in my exciting career. I still felt like an academic because researching artists and paintings was an important part of my work. I found that I had a really good eye. I also had to learn the ins and outs of the market and how to bid at auctions. As the demand for nineteenth-century American art grew, the prices skyrocketed, and I never wanted to be the uninformed buyer who overpaid.

Case in point . . . Frederic Edwin Church, a significant figure in the Hudson River School of American landscape artists, painted one of his greatest works, *The Icebergs*, in 1861. The *New-York Daily Tribune* called it the "most splendid work of art that has yet been produced in this country," and then it disappeared for seventy-eight years until, inexplicably, it turned up in a home for delinquent boys in England. There was great excitement when Sotheby's Parke-Bernet announced it would come up at auction in 1979.

I was ready to bid up to $1 million, which would have been the highest price ever paid for an American painting. I didn't think it was worth more than that. But "worth" is subjective. Lamar Hunt paid $2.5 million, setting a record. I doubted he would be able to sell it at that price in the future.

The fact that I was bidding on blockbuster paintings signaled that I was a serious player, and buyers and sellers started coming to me to see if I could help them find whatever elusive work they coveted. Or, they might have been ready to sell the family's Martin Johnson Heade. My benefactor didn't mind if I had other clients as long as he came first, so I formed an art advisory company I called Arcadia Inc.—a name that evoked the beautiful landscapes in the Hudson River School paintings I often bought and sold—and became a consultant for the top-ten collectors of nineteenth-century American art.

I was so happy at work that I found it difficult to face unhappier realities at home. Everything looked perfect, but Lon and I had to face the fact that we were growing apart. We'd shared fourteen wonderful years together until we found ourselves moving in different directions. Our life wasn't unpleasant, and we weren't fighting, but we both were preoccupied with our careers. Lon was an important figure in the financial world in Washington, and I was making a lot of money—and having a lot of fun—in a profession that I loved.

He needed a more traditional wife who could manage the household, entertain his clients, go with him on golf trips and wine tours, and be a constant source of support. To be honest, I needed a wife, too!

Looking back, I realize that we were part of a trend or, more accurately, a movement. Many couples reached this existential turning point in 1979, the year of the historic divorce boom. In 1969, the divorce rate was 3.2 divorces per 1,000 Americans. Ten years later, it was up to 5.3, the highest it has ever been, including today.

Women were questioning their roles and men's expectations of those roles and concluded that no one should have to relinquish their identity or modify a lifestyle for a partner. It's sad when a long-standing marriage falls apart, but the truth is that divorce can lead to a better situation for everyone concerned. I wish I had known about my mother's divorce then (she didn't tell me until I was forty) because her story would have been inspiring, but she was very supportive of our decision because she knew my career was important to me and how unhappy I would be if I had to give it up. She cared about Lon and his happiness, too, and always treated him like a member of the family.

Lon and I acknowledged our differences and moved forward, continuing as friends and co-parents in the most amicable, responsible, and respectful ways. Whitney's well-being was our only consideration. We wanted our son to feel loved and supported by both of us, so our approach to divorce was "conscious uncoupling" decades before Gwyneth Paltrow popularized the term. I'd even go so far as to say that we became better friends after our marriage ended.

We established separate households in the same part of Georgetown, where Whitney was still in school, and each home was equipped with everything he needed. He stayed with me on Mondays and Tuesdays and with Lon on Wednesdays and Thursdays, and we alternated weekends. Lon and I were very accommodating. For example, if Whitney was scheduled to be with me on Father's

Day, I would never prevent him from spending the day with Lon. If either of us had to travel, we'd send a car to pick up one of Whitney's grandmothers, and they'd move into the house and take care of him. More important, Lon and I were equally present in his life. We attended parent-teacher conferences together and spoke on the phone practically every day. Whitney never had to choose between us, so he grew up feeling close to both his parents. I know that's not typical in most divorces, and I'm happy we were able to maintain such a positive relationship.

I attended an event at the Smithsonian National Air and Space Museum, and I was seated with Alan Shepard, the astronaut who was the first American to travel into space, in 1961, and the fifth man to walk on the moon a few years later. Alan was one of the original Mercury Seven, NASA's men with "the right stuff." Maybe there was a bit of a flirtation between us, but I had one thought: Whitney had to meet this American hero.

I asked Alan if he would like to come to the house to meet my son, and he graciously agreed. I prepared Whitney for the big moment, reminding him of the moon landing, the ticker tape parades, and how significant it was that he was about to spend time with a *real* astronaut. How many seven-year-olds had that opportunity?

The two of them met, and Alan kept the conversation interesting. Then, the big moment. Alan took off his watch and said to Whitney, "This watch has been to the moon. Would you like to try it on?"

"No, thanks. I've got to go out and play," said the seven-year-old with more important things to do. Boys will be boys, even when there's an astronaut in the room.

Our circle expanded when a young man named Michael Maroney came into our lives. He was a close friend who helped me with my business and so much more. He owned a town house in Georgetown, but when I moved into my new place, which had five floors and a separate apartment, he moved into our extra apartment and became indispensable in a dozen ways. In an interesting footnote, he rented the apartment in his town house to a young man named Mohamed Hadid, who managed a used car lot on Wisconsin Avenue—who later became the father of Bella and Gigi Hadid.

In addition to helping me run my business, Michael was a gourmet chef. He made us Peking duck one Thanksgiving, and I don't know of many people who can do that at home. He spoke several languages, was knowledgeable about everything, and was a great companion to Whitney and a dear friend to me.

Michael had a substantial trust fund and well-to-do parents who disowned him when they found out he was gay. Why did it matter? Their behavior seemed so heartless and cruel to me because Michael was so lovable. Whitney and I happily stepped in to become his family—my mother, too, because she adored him. He also had a coterie of friends in Washington, mostly charming and interesting gay men who were lawyers, the heads of PR firms, and lobbyists, so they knew the real scoop of what was going on in politics.

Michael was our rock . . . until he started to feel sick, and no one could tell him why. I appealed to our family friend, Senator John Warner, to get him into the National Institutes of Health to see if he could be diagnosed and treated. My mother and I sat at his bedside every day, helpless as his mysterious condition got worse.

Michael died there in February 1980, right before AIDS was identified as the plague affecting gay men. Within a year, all the bright and promising men in Michael's circle succumbed to AIDS, as well. I'm still sad when I remember what a bright light Michael was in our lives and how tragically that light was extinguished.

In 2019, I rode on the Bravo float at World Pride Day in New York City, and I know Michael would have been tickled to see me wearing an enormous rainbow headdress . . . and celebrating him.

Five

I was only twenty when I went from being a daughter to a wife and got married—that's what most women did then. I took everything seriously and was dedicated to being ambitious and making something of myself, so there was no tomfoolery in my life. Now, I was single and successful at the best possible time: the eighties!

Two things were true in the eighties: greed was good, and girls just wanted to have fun. Considering the severe economic recession that kicked off the beginning of the decade, it was amazing how much money poured into the art market. Collectors, especially the newly minted ones from the financial sector, viewed art as another asset and spent like drunken sailors on a furlough.

Art dealers were ecstatic because there was so much money to be made. The major players in my field were all men, and, for several reasons, they weren't thrilled when I arrived on the scene. My biggest and most obvious flaw was that I was a young woman. They turned a blind eye to my substantial academic credentials, including a double master's degree in art history and archaeology, and saw my femininity as a threat. To make matters worse (from their points of view), I traveled in the same social circles as my clients, which gave me easier access to collectors.

I didn't play by their rules. My best advantage was Barbara, one of the most knowledgeable experts in the art world. Other dealers had to rely on their wits or hire outside consultants, but Barbara was my partner, and she was brilliant. She was only a call away for every important decision.

I didn't have a gallery—I displayed paintings in my home in Georgetown, a perfect backdrop for artwork. The two-story living room had exposed brick walls that could accommodate oversize pictures, and I furnished the room with white contemporary pieces and family antiques. Nothing about the space was commercial, so when a client came over, the process of buying and selling was more personal and elevated. It was also more discreet. Galleries are very public, but no one could see the clients who visited my home.

Occasionally, a client crossed the line between professional and personal behavior. Dealers may have seen my femininity as a threat, but some clients saw it as an invitation. I'm thinking of one horrible, self-satisfied little man who was in the process of founding a museum in a major city. He kept making inappropriate comments, thinking I would tolerate whatever he said or did because he was an important collector. I tried to laugh off his advances and get back to business, even when he surprised me with an unwelcome kiss. Women in the workplace had to tolerate this kind of behavior constantly. Instead of calling it out, we tried to outsmart the offenders and stay one step ahead of them.

When the man in question insisted that I meet him for lunch, I brought in the troops—my mother—knowing that nothing inappropriate would happen while she was at the table. Midway through the meal, the fool announced he wanted to marry me. I looked at him in shock, and my mother looked at me in utter disbelief. That wasn't going to happen . . . ever.

I evaded his proposal that day but, in our subsequent encounters, left him with a parting gift. He was one of Ronald Reagan's biggest donors and had been promised an appointment but didn't know what to request. Of course he didn't. I suggested the lofty title "ambassador at large for cultural affairs," which made him even more insufferable. But at least I never had to call him husband.

I navigated the land mines that came my way, knowing I couldn't afford to make a major mistake because the art community was very small. Believe me, they were watching my every move. I'd study a painting's condition report and then examine the work in person because it's always best to see it with your own eyes. You can have a beautiful painting by a well-known artist, but if the condition is compromised—if there's paint loss, overpainting, or if a face has been redone—the work's value drops.

And God forbid it turned out to be a fake.

I remember traveling to London to see an important painting. It was beautiful, but the signature didn't look right to me. The auction house insisted it was authentic, but they sometimes make mistakes. I still had my doubts, so I took a picture of the signature and sent it to Barbara. She confirmed that my instinct was correct. It was a good painting, but a good painting by someone else, not the artist in question, which made it worthless.

Finding and assessing the art was only part of the job. I had to do a lot of groundwork to stay on top, and I developed my own tricks of the trade. I had loaned a painting to the White House for an exhibition, and the happy result of the experience was that I ended up with a pad of White House labels—a gift from my old friend Clem Conger, who was White House curator from 1970 to 1986. I frequently traveled back and forth between Washington, DC, and New York on the Eastern shuttle and usually hand-carried a small painting. All I had to do was attach the label that read "White House" to the package, and the flight attendants treated it like a VIP and did everything but serve it drinks.

I also came up with a novel advertising strategy. The art world had several glossy trade magazines at the time—*The Magazine Antiques*, *Art and Antiques*, and others—where dealers advertised the paintings they hoped to sell. I did just the opposite. I would place an ad with the image of a painting that I had *sold*—and I always splurged on a full-page ad, never a half-page—accompanied by the artist's name and the words "Recently sold to a private client." It was reverse psychology at its best: collectors reading the ad realized they had missed out on an excellent buy, prompting them to contact me to find something similar for their collections. Inquiries came from everywhere, and I was in perpetual motion, meeting the demand.

Recently, I came across my journal from 1980. The month of December was a blur of activities. I was either on the Eastern shuttle—which offered flights from Washington, DC, to New York every hour on the hour—or flying to and from Europe on the Concorde, as if it were a bus. A meeting at the Terra Museum in Chicago, an auction at Christie's in New York, a visit with collectors in Dallas, and lunch with Jack Nicholson in Los Angeles . . .

Yes, *that* Jack Nicholson. Members of the Hollywood establishment, including actor Edward G. Robinson and producer Ray Stark, were serious art lovers who amassed museum-worthy collections. But some of the most interesting, eclectic, and forward-thinking collectors were the young rebels from the new Hollywood, and Jack Nicholson was the leader of the pack. Whenever I was in LA, I'd visit Jack and show him transparencies of works that might interest him.

Jack was a good host, but this was the eighties, so the refreshments on offer tended to be the mind-altering kind. I always declined, but one day, I said, "I'll take a martini." He looked at me in that sly Jack Nicholson way and said, "Martinis, nobody drinks martinis. . . . I don't keep *gin*." I guess my request was too old-school for a hipster like Jack.

He was such an attractive man, clearly all male, all the time, that I had to remind myself to behave professionally. Fortunately, my better angels won; we kept our relationship platonic, and I sold him several paintings.

My better angels were tested again when I flew to London in that same busy December to have lunch with Baron Hans Heinrich Thyssen-Bornemisza. "Heini" was the world's greatest art collector, second only to Queen Elizabeth. Fueled by the vast fortune he had amassed in steel and armaments, he acquired hundreds of important artworks, from Old Masters to Impressionists. He also collected antique furniture and decorative objects. And now, he decided he might be interested in nineteenth-century American art.

When Barbara and I met with Heini and his wife, Denise, he said that he had a surprise for us. Suddenly, a servant interrupted our lunch, announcing, "Jack is here."

There's only one Jack. In walked Jack Nicholson, who needed no introduction.

He was friends with Heini, and we, of course, knew each other. Jack joined us for lunch and wasted no time chastising Heini for being *way* behind the times in collecting American art. But— acknowledging me and Barbara—he added that Heini was in good hands because he was sitting with the best dealer and the best scholar. Jack can be very persuasive, and I think he played a part in convincing Heini to start buying American art, which was a good development for our company. Heini immediately made plans to fly us to the Villa Favorita, his palatial home outside of Lugano, Switzerland, where his treasures were kept.

Heini was famous for his charm, which may explain why he was on his fourth marriage. When we had the opportunity to spend time together, he explained that Denise was his wife in name only and it had been that way between them for several years. She had a very public affair with his former art dealer, Franco Rappetti, who committed suicide in 1978 by jumping out of a window. Heini was getting a divorce and considered himself a free man.

The temptation to jump into a flirtation was strong, but I was preoccupied with my business and, of course, with Whitney, who was getting older and was all wrapped up in being a teenager. He enjoyed sports—especially tennis, baseball, and golf—and he loved to write, draw, and play the classical guitar. He was also showing early signs of being an entrepreneur. He cofounded a student newspaper guide for local entertainment, from movies to where to meet girls. He was confident, popular, and secure in his two homes.

I have no explanation other than temporary insanity for why I thought it would be a good idea to celebrate Whitney's birthday by taking my thirteen-year-old son and ten of his friends to a Rolling Stones concert in Philadelphia. I hired a van to transport us to JFK Stadium on a blistering hot day in September. Ninety thousand other fans had the same idea. As we crowded into the stadium, I remembered chaperoning my college students on their European art tour and how it was like herding cats. I suspected herding tweens would be much worse, and I was so right.

I led them to our seats, which were in a box very close to the stage. Immediately, one of the girls announced that she had to go to the restroom. I had no choice but to go with her, so I told the other kids to stay put. Why did I think they would listen? When we got back, they were gone, and I had no idea where they went. I grabbed the girl (I didn't want to lose another one), and we set out on the

Herculean task of finding my missing charges in the raucous crowd. Failure was not an option.

But the search was fruitless, and I was out of my mind with worry. What would I tell their parents? When the Stones finally came out, they put on quite a show, but I was distracted by the little voice in my head saying, *Never, ever again*. Eventually, the bedraggled prodigals returned. They had been standing right in front of the stage, easy targets for the firefighters who sprayed water to keep the audience away from the talent. The kids thought the water felt good, and it probably did because it was hot enough to fry the proverbial egg in that stadium. I didn't rest until I corralled the pack into the van and locked the doors. Motherhood had its challenges.

So did the art business. In 1981, I traveled to St. Louis for an event honoring Heini at the city's art museum. Just as I arrived at the entrance to my hotel—I was literally standing at the door—I heard a series of huge explosions and screams coming from inside. It felt like the world was ending. Smoke and water poured out of the building. Terrified that a bomb had gone off, I joined the crowd running in the opposite direction.

It wasn't a bomb, but it was just as lethal. A walkway collapsed inside the Hyatt hotel, killing 114 people and injuring another 216. I was seconds away from being one of those poor victims—a sobering thought.

I was shaken by my brush with death. Then something even more frightening happened. I was home in Georgetown one night when the doorbell rang. I opened the door and saw Roy Cohn, the ruthless and unprincipled lawyer who was best known for prosecuting Julius and Ethel Rosenberg, conducting witch hunts for Joseph McCarthy, and acting as a nefarious consigliere for various politicos and businessmen, standing right there in front of me on my stoop.

I had seen him in the newspaper and on television, but he was even more reptilian in person.

He sensed that I was shocked and skipped any niceties—although I can't imagine that *nicety* was a word in his vocabulary—and got straight to the point. He was here on behalf of an art dealer named Andrew Crispo, and he had come to threaten me.

A little background on Crispo to introduce the man behind the threat. His name may sound familiar because he was linked to the "death mask murder," a notorious case in 1985, when a young man's body, his face covered with a leather S & M mask, was discovered in Rockland County, New York. Eigil Dag Vesti's death was attributed to a night of sex play gone wrong—a night he had spent with Crispo and his assistant, Bernard LeGeros. While LeGeros confessed to shooting Vesti, he claimed that Crispo ordered him to do it. In the absence of corroborating evidence, Crispo was not charged in the case, but LeGeros was convicted and given the maximum sentence of twenty-five years to life.

Crispo had another well-publicized run-in with the law when he was convicted of tax evasion and sent to prison. But before any of this happened, Crispo was a prominent Upper East Side art dealer with a hot gallery patronized by celebrities. Heini Thyssen was one of his best clients, a real cash cow. When Heini started buying paintings from me, Crispo saw money slipping out of his hands and called on his friend Roy Cohn to put a stop to it.

Cohn looked me in the eye and said, "If you don't stop selling paintings to him [meaning Heini], I don't know what will happen to your young son."

I remembered stories about Crispo had circulated when Franco Rappetti "jumped" out of a window and fell seventeen stories to his death. Rumor had it that Rappetti, who had been Heini's art dealer before Crispo, tried to shake down his rival for a kickback. Did he fall, or was he pushed because he was getting in Crispo's way?

Whatever had happened, I understood that Crispo was danger-ous, and I took Cohn's threat very seriously. I had to move quickly to protect Whitney. I decided the best course of action was to leave the country and go to the Mediterranean, where Cohn and his goons couldn't find me. I chartered a yacht and took Whitney, his friend, and my assistant on a very long and leisurely cruise around the coasts of France and Italy. Eventually, I stopped being scared and started to enjoy the trip.

We spent the summer visiting little fishing villages and islands and made a memorable stop in Monaco. I wanted Whitney to see the casino because it's so beautiful. He and his friend were underage, but they were tall and looked older, so we got in without any prob-lem. At one point that evening, I went to the ladies' room, but when I returned, I couldn't find Whitney anywhere . . . until I checked the gaming tables. He was front and center at a blackjack table with a pile of chips in front of him.

Whitney looked *very* happy because he had already won $20,000! I'm sure he thought his big haul was based on his skill and saw the experience as the beginning of a lucrative career, but I nipped that thought in the bud and made him invest the money. When I think of that summer, I remember Whitney and his chips—not the salted kind!

Flash forward—Lon took Whitney on a business trip to Las Vegas. Whitney was approaching his sixteenth birthday, and all he wanted was a car, which his father and I had refused to buy for a teenager with no driving experience. He took one look at the black-jack table and saw the future.

"I know how to play blackjack," he assured Lon. "I'll buy my own car." He sat down at the table and proceeded to lose *all* his money, and thankfully his gambling career was over.

Six

———⟡———

I came home from our yachting trip with a clearer perspective. Heini Thyssen and I remained friends, but he was in the rearview mirror as a client—there was too much danger around him, and life was too short to make it even shorter by becoming a target for people like Roy Cohn. Thankfully, I never heard from that despicable man again.

My other clients kept me busy, and I continued to travel back and forth to Europe. Whenever possible, I brought Whitney with me, something I did even when he was a child, because I thought it was important for him to learn at an early age about different cultures, foods, and ways of life.

We had a memorable encounter during one of our flights on the Concorde. Before our trip, we had just watched a terrifying television movie called *The Day After*, which told the story of the United States on the brink of nuclear war. It was the most-watched movie in television history, and everyone was talking about the threat of "nuclear winter," the aftermath of a nuclear blast. The subject was so timely and important that ABC aired a news special with a panel of experts, including Dr. Henry Kissinger, to discuss the threat.

When we boarded the Concorde that day, Dr. Kissinger himself sat next to us! It was as if he had stepped out of the television to speak to us personally. He was so kind. He talked to us at length about the program and tried to allay our fears, promising the US government would do everything to make sure that nuclear winter never happened. We definitely felt better. And if I thought that travel was educational before . . . after our experience with Dr. Kissinger, I was even more convinced!

I saw Dr. Kissinger again two years later at one of the greatest parties of all time—Marylou Whitney's Derby Eve event in 1985. Marylou was America's preeminent horsewoman and a fixture in society, and her party, celebrating the 111th running of the Kentucky Derby, was a coveted invitation for horse people and celebrities from around the globe and a showstopper from start to finish. That year, the theme was "Rhapsody in Blue," and Marylou transformed Maple Hill at the Whitney Stables Farm into a fantasy setting, complete with a bridge built across the Olympic-size pool, set with dining tables. The pool was filled with lifelike swans fashioned from white flowers. A fleet of servers greeted the guests as they arrived—including the aforementioned Henry Kissinger, Walter Cronkite, Diane Sawyer, Ginger Rogers, Esther Williams, Gregory and Veronique Peck, Rock Hudson, and scores of other notables.

Rock Hudson stood out that night because he was so strikingly, seriously handsome, but also because he seemed a little unwell and thinner than usual. Two months later, Hudson collapsed in Paris, and his publicist confirmed that he had AIDS. He died later that year. The fact that he was brave enough to acknowledge he had the disease helped to change the way AIDS was perceived by the public—and with greater understanding and acceptance came more funding for HIV research, which led to breakthrough treatments.

I thought about my friend Michael and his friends and wished they could have been helped by these lifesaving developments.

I started to feel that I needed a reset. I loved my town house, but I was at a point in my life when I no longer needed a vast open space to display art. I preferred something cozier and more European, more of a pied-à-terre, and I found it in an early-nineteenth-century town house that retained most of its original—and very quirky—details. It had wood plank floors, rooms that were intimate in scale, and lots of *character*, the word we use to describe houses that present design challenges. My biggest problem was figuring out how to edit my possessions. The big paintings were the first to go. I selected a deep, rich red for the walls and filled the rooms with my best English and French antiques.

A dynamic new man in my life was another pleasant distraction. I spent a good deal of time in Palm Beach, where friends introduced me to an international businessman named Robert de Balkany, and I succumbed to the charms of an art connoisseur. Show me a man who hangs the works of Tintoretto and Van Dyck on the walls of his Hôtel Particulier in Paris and owns a collection of 265 priceless antique clocks, and I'm smitten.

Robert had other attributes. He was a visionary businessman who was smart, handsome, urbane, and very successful. As a property developer, he introduced the French to American-styled shopping malls (which may or may not have been a good thing). He was wild about polo, a sport I enjoyed watching; maintained a stable of ponies in Wellington, Florida; and had a private polo field at his château in Paris. He lived like a king, an image that was burnished by his marriage to Princess Marie Gabrielle of Savoy, whose father was the last king of Italy. Their relationship had soured, and a divorce was in the works, leaving Robert free to embrace life as a jet-setting bachelor.

Our relationship was right out of a romance novel. I'd meet him in Paris, Palm Beach, or on his yacht, where he worked hard (he was always in the middle of a big deal) and played hard. But he wasn't all playboy bluster. Robert's mansion housed priceless treasures, and he was a passionate art collector who was knowledgeable about everything he acquired. He taught me so much about the decorative arts, especially how to surround yourself with artwork and antiques without making it seem as if you lived in a museum.

However, some of Robert's kingly ideas were old-fashioned or just plain wrong. My parents taught me to respect the people who worked in our home. They were employees providing valuable services, and, as in any other workplace, there were rules of civility that applied to both sides. Robert didn't see it that way. The people on his domestic staff were servants at his beck and call, subject to his imperious whims. He was often rude and aggressive, prompting one detractor to point out that there was a reason his polo pony colors were black and blue—his tyrannical behavior was bruising.

Robert never treated me that way—I wouldn't have tolerated it for a minute. But I think we're defined by how we treat others, especially those who are less powerful and have no recourse, so I decided to stop seeing him.

By 1989, I felt that a chapter in my life—like the wild and exhilarating decade—was coming to a close. The art market was changing, and not in my favor. There was an influx of big buyers from Japan, and they preferred works by the French Impressionists and Post-Impressionists. That market soared, but the demand for American art fizzled, and just like that, my area of expertise was no longer in fashion. I had the opportunity to sell some French paintings privately, but my heart wasn't in it.

My adventures in the art world had been heady, from breaking the sound barrier on the Concorde to attending one of the most magnificent parties I've ever experienced—and I've attended a zillion events all over the world. This one, a black-tie dinner at Versailles, was the pièce de résistance. The occasion was a celebration of an exhibition of French and American Impressionist art, shown together for the first time, and the guests, mostly French aristocrats, were beyond glamorous. They arrived in a procession of limousines and swept through the historic palace doors. Beautiful women, dressed in ball gowns and bedecked with tiaras and glittering jewels, could have come straight from the court of Louis XIV.

We dined in the Hall of Mirrors, the most famous room in the palace. Designed by the royal architect Jules Hardouin-Mansart in 1678, the room features 43 chandeliers and 357 mirrors. As beautiful as the guests were in real life, they looked like works of art in the reflections that lined the room. After dinner, we were led through the gardens to the Queen's Theatre, one of the two theaters on the palace grounds. In this magical space, commissioned by Marie Antoinette, we were entertained by a classical music concert. I felt like I was at the center of a glorious tableaux from another time.

Eventually, the clock strikes twelve for every Cinderella. I was ready to move on, even if I didn't know what might come next. To draw a hard line between my old life and my (uncertain) future, I pulled out my Rolodex—the biggest one you've ever seen—and hand-shredded all my contacts and collector files. It was a symbolic gesture that I regret now. I should have kept it—like a relic—but I wanted a clean break and a new beginning.

Ask Me Anything:

Art Edition

Do you have a favorite artist?
No, I love too many from all different centuries to be able to name just one.

What's the best way to start collecting art?
I think the first tenet of buying art is to figure out what you love and what inspires you. Whether you're shopping at a flea market or an auction house, you have to feel a connection to the object and believe it will enhance your life in some way. Every time you look at it, you want to be thrilled that you got it. You should educate yourself by learning more about a period you like and the artists of that period. Visit museums and galleries and read auction catalogs. Even if you're interested in contemporary art or artists who are lesser known (or not known at all), research will help you to be more knowledgeable.

Do you have a prized possession?
Yes, Whitney.

Seven

A hoy! Who knew that this word, a greeting exchanged by sailors everywhere, would become a part of my daily vocabulary? Not me, when I stopped working as an art adviser and settled into a new life. Whitney had graduated from college and was studying at Oxford, and I had an active social life. I met some very interesting men, but I'm not naming names because most of them have died, or their wives wouldn't want me to mention them. I remember someone telling me that statistics suggested I would have a better chance of being killed by a terrorist than I would to ever find another husband. Then, a friend introduced me to Ed Fleming.

Ed was six foot five, movie-star handsome, a psychiatrist, and a successful entrepreneur. He owned almost a hundred psychiatric hospitals, which he cleverly rebranded as the Psychiatric Institutes of America to meet the booming demand for private rehab facilities in the drug-fueled eighties. They became so popular that he later sold the company for $400 million. On top of that, he lived in the prettiest town house in Georgetown, *and* he had just gotten a divorce, which made him the most eligible bachelor in Washington.

We had dinner together a few times—once on his motor yacht, the *Silver Cloud*—which was one of the nicest boats I'd been on, and by this point in my life, I'd been on quite a few. Ed shared my interest in art and antiques (he once owned an antiques store with his first wife), my passion for professional-level croquet, and my reverence for family genealogy. He was a direct descendant of Robert E. Lee, and his other ancestors included Pocahontas, whose portrait he proudly displayed on his yacht. Best of all, I truly enjoyed his company.

On one of our dates, he announced that he planned to circumnavigate the country on his boat via the Loop, a six-thousand-mile trip through the eastern United States and Canada's interconnected waterways, including the Atlantic Ocean and the Great Lakes. Completing the Loop was a badge of honor for serious yachtsmen, so it didn't surprise me that Ed had this adventure on his bucket list. What I didn't expect was for him to invite me to go with him.

My response was a hard no. My mother was still alive, and she thought a woman was "loose" if she had pierced ears. What would she think of a woman who lived with a man without the benefit of wedlock? I didn't want to find out, so I told Ed it wouldn't be appropriate.

Ed had a quick answer. "Well," he said, "let's get married; then it will be appropriate."

I don't know why, but his sudden proposal made sense in a crazy way. I've always been a risk-taker, so I thought, *Why not?* I've never been one to turn down an adventure, especially one that involves a handsome man, a yacht, and a French chef. After a quick ceremony on the *Silver Cloud*, I was a married woman—again—and planning a honeymoon cruise on what one magazine cleverly called our *"pied-à-mer."*

We idled in Virginia while we planned the trip. One day, I attended a meeting hosted by the Colonial Dames of America in

Middleburg—my mother insisted that I join the group because of my family's Revolutionary War history. I also belonged to the United Daughters of the Confederacy—that was the Dey legacy—so every side got equal time. I sat between two women who could have been mother and daughter or companionable maiden aunts. It was hard to tell because they were so ancient and prim that they could have come straight from a Grant Wood painting.

I told them that I had recently married and that my husband owned Annefield, a historic Federalist mansion and country estate in Virginia. One of the women recognized Ed's name and chirped, "Oh, Ed Fleming! He's a renowned cocksman."

I was shocked. Should I confirm or deny? Normally, I have a retort for everything, but hearing *that* word from a Colonial Dame, apparently a very frisky one, rendered me speechless.

Later, at tea, I found myself speaking to the other woman, and I told her I was shocked by her companion's description of my husband.

"What do you mean?" she said quizzically.

"Well, when she referred to Ed as a cocksman," I answered, forcing myself to say the word.

"No, *yachtsman*," she clarified, practically laughing her head off.

That was a relief because I couldn't figure out how that elderly dame knew so much about Ed and his talent.

Early on in our voyage, I decided that the *Silver Cloud* needed a makeover. Ed had been content with what I'll politely call spartan accommodations. But I wanted a proper home, not a bachelor pad. I asked my decorator to turn an afterdeck space into a library, complete with Chippendale chairs, wallpaper wainscotting, and a lovely Frederic Church landscape from my collection. The result was so stunning that we redecorated every room with Brunschwig & Fils fabrics, French and English antiques, and chinoiserie (from my father's travels). The master suite was resplendent in leopard, which I'm not sure the two cats we adopted in Chicago, Rambo and Kitty Kelly, found appropriate. But they did enjoy drinking out of their large Waterford water bowl.

We were always in motion, so our poor decorator had to meet us at various ports and scurry on board to do the work. He was a very good sport. I wanted the *Silver Cloud* to be beautiful and elegant and to have all the comforts of home, but I'm never happy if everything is too serious, so we added a whimsical detail.

A ship's figurehead is supposed to be a carved representation of the vessel's spirit, and most of the time, it is something from mythology, like a mermaid. We didn't have a figurehead per se, but whenever we docked, we hauled out an eye-catching painted cutout of a cow and displayed it on deck for all to see.

"It's our party cow," I explained to a journalist who was writing an article about the *Silver Cloud*'s transformation.

"After all, we're Southern," I told her. "So it's expected that we'll be a little eccentric." That cow, the least maritime figure imaginable, got a lot of attention when people noticed it "grazing" on our deck.

The Loop lived up to its reputation. Traveling through the country on various waterways, which hardly seemed possible, gave me the opportunity to see places I had never seen before. We started out in Annapolis and went all the way up the Intracoastal to New York, Newport, Rhode Island, and Maine. We didn't always stop in large harbors, and some of the rural ports were real kick-off-your-shoes places that were casual and fun. We stayed in Maine for the summer, then headed for Newfoundland, Montreal, and the Thousand Islands. We made another long stop in Chicago before moving on to the newly built Tombigbee Waterway that links Tennessee to Alabama. With all our stops, it took us about a year and a half to reach the Gulf of Mexico, our last destination. Then we turned around and did the Loop a *second* time.

The world outside the boat was fascinating, but life on board was another story. In retrospect, I don't recommend marrying a man you've known for only a few weeks. Handsome can only get you so far. The more I got to know Ed—something that was bound to happen when two people live in such intimate quarters—the more I realized that we were not an ideal match.

In the plus column, he was pleasant, and he loved to read. And we both loved Spam. But it turns out that a shared passion for canned meat is not a viable foundation for a marriage. On the minus side, personal relationships were not his forte. He liked to live in his own little world. From what I could see, he had no communication with two of his children, and he was against having any guests on the yacht, including Whitney and my mother.

Remember the expression "When someone tells you who they are, believe them"? Ed told me that all psychiatrists were nuts, which was problematic because *he* was a psychiatrist *and* a psychotherapist with an MD and PhD. So, I guess that made him double nuts. Despite his degrees, he called his hospitals "loony bins," which seemed so wrong.

I also discovered that he had gout, which sounded like a malady in a costume drama. Unfortunately, he loved to drink, so his gout would get worse, and he had to sit with his foot elevated. I started to wonder if I had married Henry VIII. Thank God I kept a bicycle on board. Whenever we docked, I'd jump on the bike and go exploring. If we were in a city, I'd visit museums. These small interactions with the outside world kept me sane.

Ed and I played out our various dramas on the upper deck of the *Silver Cloud*, but there were dramas belowdecks, as well.

We lost a deckhand who couldn't get along with the captain, and then tragedy struck when our cook decided to leave while we were in Demopolis, Alabama. Okay, maybe tragedy is hyperbolic, but given that Demopolis had a population of about seven thousand, it was unlikely we would find a new cook there. Imagine how I felt when I had to take over in the galley (imagine how Ed felt!) until we imported a replacement. We all have our gifts and talents. My specialty was bologna-and-cheese sandwiches with mayonnaise on Wonder bread and a side of chips. I opened the chips myself. It was a nightmare.

The weather was fine when we did the Loop—but we had a terrible experience in the Outer Hebrides, a night when my life flashed before me. In addition to owning the *Silver Cloud*, Ed kept a historic sailboat in the South of France. He persuaded me to accompany him on a sailing trip to Scotland, the only time I ventured out on that death ship. One day, the clouds gathered, the skies darkened, and the sea swelled. Ed announced gleefully that we would hit some rough weather, the kind that unleashes monstrous waves and appeals to die-hard sailors and absolutely no one else.

I should have known there might be trouble ahead when I saw the heavy straps that crisscrossed the bed in the cabin. They were meant to hold me in place so I wouldn't fall out and hurt myself during a storm. The situation was even more intense because we had our two Siamese cats with us. They had been delightful company and good sailors until now.

As the waves turned into cliffs and the ship pitched violently, Ed positioned me in the bed, tightened my straps, and gave me a stiff drink to knock me out. The poor cats had no such recourse. They expressed their terror by howling and pooping everywhere, giving new meaning to the term *scared shitless*. We survived the storm, but I never, ever, set foot on that sailboat again.

The storm was the beginning of the end for us. When Ed tried to convince me to give up my American citizenship and move to Ireland because he needed a tax haven, our voyage together was over. I missed my family, and I wanted to spend time with my mother, whose health was failing. Ed and I discussed a separation agreement, and I jumped ship.

Eight

M other always said, "Marry in haste, repent in leisure." She was so right. Agreeing to get a divorce means nothing when the correspondent has no permanent address. My real odyssey began when I tried to serve Ed with divorce papers. The man was always off on the high seas and impossible to find. At least *I* was on dry land and intended to keep it that way.

I moved to Virginia, and freedom was intoxicating. I could spend time with my mother, who really needed me. Sadly, she passed away later in 1991. I was lucky to have had so many wonderful memories of our crazy adventures. How many mothers and daughters can say that they traveled the world together, experiencing everything from grand opera to the naked, ding-dong-swinging Asaro Mudmen in Papua New Guinea? I'd like to think that I inherited her endless curiosity and enthusiasm for doing the unexpected. She was full of surprises and always took the road *less* traveled, and that's how I'll remember her.

I was also able to spend more time with Whitney and rekindle long-neglected relationships with friends. The simplest pleasures took on more meaning—driving instead of yachting to a destination.

And wearing high heels—something that never happens on a boat.

I started dating again, and one night, about a year and a half after I jumped ship, I attended an event celebrating the reopening of artist James McNeill Whistler's Peacock Room, a stunning aesthetic interior, at the Smithsonian's Freer Gallery of Art. As I admired the extraordinary painted panels and the display of Chinese blue-and-white porcelain, I bumped into Arthur Altschul, a charming man I'd known for years. Barbara had introduced us when I first started working as an art adviser. She knew him well because she taught at Barnard College, where Arthur had been chairman of the board. He was one of the country's top twenty collectors, and we were delighted to have him as a client.

In addition to being a serious collector, Arthur was a titan in the world of finance and a dedicated philanthropist. As impressive as these labels were, they didn't begin to describe the man in full. He was a gentleman—warm, witty, and blessed with impeccable manners. He treated everyone with equal respect and consideration, unlike some who had his advantages and resources but exploited their privilege and power (Robert de Balkany comes to mind).

Although Arthur came from generations of wealth and influence, he wore his advantages lightly. His mother, Helen Lehman Goodhart Altschul, was the granddaughter of one of the three founders of Lehman Brothers, while his father, Frank Altschul, was the head of General American Investors Company and the founder of the Overbrook Management Corporation. In every generation, the Altschuls and the Lehmans before them had a history of sharing their good fortune with others. Success and philanthropy were in Arthur's DNA, and so was integrity: as he told his children, "Be honest, fair, and generous in all of your dealings."

He respected tradition but was fiercely independent and did things *his* way. After graduating from Yale in 1943, he served in the

Marines from 1943 to 1945. Starting in 1946, he demonstrated his lifelong talent for mastering a broad range of subjects by working as a reporter for the *New York Times*. In one humorous article, he described the woes of a property master whose duties included finding a dogsled on wheels, five harnessed dogs, and a miniature piano for the opening of the wacky and unpredictable *The Milton Berle Show*.

He interviewed comedy legend Jack Benny about his impending transition from radio to television, a move that was considered risky, and reported that "the amiable tightwad doesn't give the impression of being a bit disturbed." On a more serious note, he reported on the Atomic Energy Commission's heated negotiations with the Soviet Union over a comprehensive system of controls for the newly invented atomic bomb.

Arthur could have had a career in journalism or anything else that captured his interest, but, eventually, he pivoted to finance and started working at Lehman, then moved to Goldman Sachs. His rise was meteoric, and he was a partner there for more than forty years. He also headed Overbrook Management Corporation, the Altschul family office.

But Arthur's real passion was art: it was the air he breathed. His collection was vast, and every acquisition reflected his personal taste. He bought works by the Neo-impressionists, the Pointillists, the Nabis, and the Ashcan School because he loved them, and it didn't matter to him what other people thought or what the market said he should buy. He was more interested in peeking behind the canvas to learn as much as possible about the artists and their worlds. He wanted everyone to have access to art and made that possible by supporting museums with both his money and his wise counsel, serving on the boards of the Metropolitan Museum of Art, the Whitney, the National Gallery, and the Yale University Art Gallery.

How could I not admire Arthur? I was so happy to see him that night at the Smithsonian. He must have felt the same way about me because his first words were, "I've been trying to get in touch with you, but your number isn't listed." I explained that I had been on a boat for what seemed like *forever*.

He got right to the point. "Well," he said, "I've gotten a divorce since I saw you last. How about you?" I told him I was in the process of getting a divorce, although I explained that God knows how long *that* would take while the Sinbad I married was off sailing the seven seas.

We looked at each other, and a light bulb went off. Arthur and I were single and available at the same time! The frisson of interest—that sense of "what if" that had always run like a current through our previous encounters—was now front and center, and we were free to give in to our mutual attraction. He immediately invited me to come to New York the following weekend to go with him to an art opening. I can't remember whether it was John Singer Sargent or Martin Johnson Heade, but I have perfect recall about the wonderful evening we spent together—great art (whoever it was), martinis, and dinner at 21 Club. We didn't want it to end.

I was supposed to go back to Virginia the next day. Instead, Arthur invited me to spend the weekend at Overbrook Farm, his home in Connecticut. We drove there together, learning more about what we had in common and how we differed. Arthur told me that his family had not been accepted by New York society in the past. It didn't matter that they were important in the financial world, dedicated leaders of government, and paragons of the community. Doors were closed to the family—and even now stayed closed—because they were Jewish.

It didn't make any sense to me. Arthur's uncle Herbert Lehman was, at various times, the governor of New York, a US senator, a social reformer, and a philanthropist who transformed New York with life-enhancing gifts, such as the Central Park Zoo. Arthur's father, another substantial figure in New York banking, who introduced Lazard Fréres to America, suffered slights, large and small, and was denied membership at a country club, a problem he solved by building his own three-hundred-acre country club in Connecticut. Still . . .

Arthur explained that some of those anti-Semitic prejudices carried over to today, and he had experienced them firsthand. He couldn't join the Knickerbocker Club, a WASP bastion. His perspective was new to me, and I was moved by the stories he told. By virtue of my birth, I was a quintessential WASP, a daughter of the American Revolution and a Colonial Dame, and to some members of my family, these genealogical connections were sacrosanct. My parents, on the other hand, were more sophisticated and believed in inclusivity and meritocracy, and they sent me to schools that reinforced their beliefs. I was lucky to have that kind of enlightened upbringing. Religious discrimination—any kind of discrimination, for that matter—was wrong.

I knew that Arthur and his family had suffered in other ways. In 1936, when Arthur was sixteen, his older brother, Charles, left New York after a family vacation to head back to California, where he studied aeronautical engineering. The plane crashed in Arkansas, killing everyone on board.

Twenty-five years later, tragedy struck again. Arthur married Stephanie Wagner in 1956. The happy couple had two sons, Stephen and Charles, and were expecting their third child in a few months. On a sunny spring day in April 1961, Stephanie boarded a small air taxi flying from New York City to Southampton. The pilot reported a problem a short time after takeoff, and within seconds, the plane crashed in the backyard of a house in Queens and exploded in flames. Stephanie, two other women, and the pilot were killed instantly. The emotional wounds of that experience were deep for Arthur and his two young boys.

Several years later, in 1963, Arthur married Siri von Reis, an accomplished young woman who was a botanist and a research fellow at the Harvard Botanical Museum, a poet, and an art collector. They had three children: Arthur Jr., Emily, and Serena. They divorced in 1972. He married Diana Landreth Childs in 1980, but their marriage ended in divorce a few years later, and now he was free.

When we arrived at Overbrook Farm, I think we were both curious about what might happen next between us. But first, the tour. The farm had been in the Altschul family for decades and was a magnificent property that included an enormous main house, a smaller house built by the noted architect Edward Durell Stone, a barn, stables, a chicken farm large enough to comfortably accommodate six hundred chickens, a pool, double tennis courts, and the requisite Connecticut babbling brook. The main house had great bones but was a hodgepodge of furniture from different decades and three different wives. The library, where Arthur spent most of his time, was an impressive transplant from an English country house.

We weren't the only ones in residence that weekend. Arthur's son Charles was visiting with a friend, and they joined us for dinner. Charles was very personable, and we spent a lovely evening together. Arthur had a wonderful relationship with Charles and, as I later discovered, with all of his children—which was such a refreshing change from Ed Fleming, who didn't speak to two of his three children.

Eventually, I said good night and retired to my room. It had been a long day, and I welcomed the chance to take a hot bath and slip under the covers.

Then, a soft knock at the door. Arthur. He came in and asked, "Do you want me to read you a bedtime story?"

I couldn't wait to hear that story, but I'm keeping the ending to myself!

Nine

My weekend in Connecticut turned into two weeks because Arthur and I were reluctant to part. We had an easy, comfortable rapport. He could *always* make me laugh. And he was brilliant. He had that wonderful kind of plummy, almost English way of speaking, and he loved to read and study and talk to me about what he learned.

Something special was happening between us, and it was happening fast, so it was a sad day when I had to go back to Virginia to check on my house and Rambo and Kitty Kelly, my two cats who survived the hellish night at sea. When I saw that my housekeeper had everything under control, I rushed right back to Arthur, and that's how we lived for the next few months, going back and forth as often as possible.

Eventually, Arthur suggested I get rid of my house in Virginia and stay with him. Instead of giving in to my impulse to behave like a lovesick teenager, I decided to be practical. In my most adult voice, I explained that my mission was to get a divorce, and my lawyers were in Virginia. I should stay close to them and focus on the job at hand. Arthur wasn't having any of that. "There are planes," he pointed out, arguing his case. He was very persuasive—and I was falling in love—so I packed up my furniture, art, and everything else in the house—and my cats—and moved in with him.

Arthur's New York apartment, my new home, occupied the entire twelfth floor at 993 Fifth Avenue, a building designed by the eminent architect Emery Roth, who also created the San Remo and the Beresford on Central Park West and the Ritz Tower on Park Avenue. The twelve-room, 5,200-square-foot apartment overlooked the Metropolitan Museum of Art and Central Park and featured grand spaces, a woodburning fireplace, and planting terraces. But the decor, if you can call it that, was horrendous—like Overbrook Farm, a cacophony of furniture, clashing wallpaper, and questionable design choices leftover from his previous wives.

Actually, they hadn't left much, and what was there looked like the mismatched pieces destined for a graduate student's apartment. Arthur was blind to his exes' discordant legacies because he was only interested in showcasing his collection. Paintings covered every wall, and the ones on view were the tip of the iceberg. He had turned a large room into a state-of-the-art, climate-controlled storage space for his art, where hundreds of paintings were stored on racks and maintained by an on-site curator.

Periodically, Arthur would disappear into the "closet" and emerge with another masterpiece that *had* to be hung. But where? We already looked like upscale hoarders. I convinced Arthur that the apartment's chaotic interior detracted from his art. The solution was to hire a decorator. Not just any decorator, but the one who was my Holy Grail: Mario Buatta, dubbed the "Prince of Chintz."

I had been following Mario's work for years and had two huge files of clippings of his work featured in interior design magazines. I admired his style—what his biographer Emily Eerdmans called

"English country house" with "a sunny optimism that is wholly American." Mario initially intended to be an architect, but he dropped out of Cooper Union after nine weeks because, as he said, "I wanted to know where the pillows went, not where the pipes went."

When he started working as an interior designer, he quickly proved that he knew how to bring a room to life from the ground up. He masterminded everything—from the walls, moldings, and columns to the decorative pillows on the sofa and the objects on the mantel—and saw to it that these details played nicely with others. His interiors served as beautiful, expressive backdrops for the people who inhabited them. They were easy to live in, *and* they made everyone look good. "Decorating isn't fashion," he said. "You're setting the stage for people to act out their lives."

When I called Mario to set up a meeting (amazingly, he was listed in the telephone book and lived only three blocks away), I thought I would be interviewing him. But it turned out that he was interviewing *me*. Mario had reached a point in his career when he could be selective about his clients. Paige Rense, the editor of *Architectural Digest*, noted that "Whenever we showed a Mario interior on the cover, newsstand sales went up." His work was on display in the homes of Henry Ford, Nelson Doubleday, Malcolm Forbes, Mariah Carey, and Billy Joel, and he was in constant demand.

It turns out I made a good impression when I pulled out my overstuffed files. Mario was incredulous.

"Can I borrow them?" he asked. He told me I had more information on him than he had on himself! I had captured his interest, so I explained what I had in mind. We were up against certain obstacles at the New York apartment, namely that Arthur didn't want busy wallpaper or anything that would detract from his art.

Mario looked around, processing the paintings that covered every wall, and said, "Well, there *are* too many paintings, but I'll try to work around them." Mario did his best to improve the apartment, never complaining when a Mary Cassatt, a Georgia O' Keeffe, or a Childe Hassam got in his way. We understood each other—probably the only people on the planet who viewed a surplus of masterpieces as a design problem to overcome—and from that moment on shared lifelong decorating adventures and a beautiful friendship.

I've always been very social, but I had trouble keeping up with Arthur. He was older than me in years—twenty-one, to be exact—but not in energy or power. If he had his way, we'd go out every night—to art openings, charity events, movie premieres, and dinner parties. He loved being with people and was indefatigable. Sometimes, we'd walk across Central Park to a restaurant on the Upper West Side and then walk all the way home through the park.

When we met Arthur's friends for dinner, I noticed that New Yorkers engaged in different kinds of conversations than the ones I was used to in the South. Northerners focus on vital statistics, asking about your job, your social network, your address, and such. They even talk about the buying and selling prices of their apartments and who got the better deal. That was all a little hard-core for me, especially the money part, and it took some getting used to, although I never jumped into the mosh pit and talked about my best deals.

Arthur also loved entertaining at home. Early in our relationship, Arthur asked me to host a holiday party for his partners at Goldman Sachs. He said *holiday*, but I heard *Christmas*—my favorite time of year. I had a vault of Christmas ornaments and decorations, some I inherited from my mother, and I asked Arthur if I could go all out and deck the halls. He was Jewish, so Christmas wasn't his holiday, but he was always up for a good party and was enthusiastic about my plans.

It was my first New York City Christmas, and maybe I got a little carried away. I ordered a gigantic tree and loaded it with so many lights that the electrical circuits in the apartment building shorted. I unpacked everything I had in storage, including my Christmas iguana (doesn't everybody have one?), which played a rousing rendition of "Feliz Navidad."

I decided to go old-school—old-*Southern*-school, that is—with the catering. There would be no trendy tuna tartare, sculpted baby vegetables, or Camembert bites—all popular choices at Manhattan soirees—at my party. Instead, the dining room table was a groaning board of pig, a "pig heaven," with platters of Smithfield ham, strips of caramelized bacon, and good old pigs in blankets with French's mustard. And what party is complete without a tower of shrimp and deviled eggs? For the finale, I served Krispy Kreme doughnuts in every variety, a guilty pleasure beloved by all.

Glorious Food, my caterer that night, warned me that no one who attended would eat *anything* from that menu, a prediction that sank like the *Titanic*. Drunk with happiness, our carb-starved guests stormed the table like it was the Bastille, and the food was gone in record time. Even though most of our guests were Yankees, by the end of the evening, any divisions between North and South had disappeared, and we were all best friends.

I think the fact that Arthur could endorse—and enjoy—an evening so different from what he was used to illustrates how compatible we were on all levels. We never argued about religion, politics, heritage, or anything else because we accepted each other for who we were—*loved* each other for who we were—and respected our differences.

Early on in our relationship, when I was still traveling to Virginia, Arthur accompanied me to a dinner party at Hickory Tree Farm, the home of Mrs. Alice duPont Mills in Middleburg. Mrs. Mills had a lifetime passion for thoroughbred horse racing and breeding, and her farm and the surrounding countryside, with its winding roads and stone buildings, were beautiful. Arthur had never been to this part of the world, which I knew and loved, and I thought he might fall in love with it too and want to get a second home there.

The dinner was lovely—everyone was beautifully dressed, and we were in this fabulous house.

"Wasn't it great?" I asked Arthur when we were on our way home.

His answer was not what I expected.

"Let's see, what did we talk about?" he said. "The price of horse feed, the best mixture of hay, the news that so-and-so's husband, who was the master of the hunt, fell off his horse, hit his head, and died. There were at least three people there with injuries—casts and whatnots—and one woman who couldn't get her foot out of the stir-rup, so her horse dragged her through the woods. If I were a farmer, I'd love it. But it's not New York."

So no, we would not get a second home in Virginia horse coun-try. I could take Arthur out of New York, but I couldn't take New York out of Arthur, and that was fine. Our differences kept life inter-esting.

It's beyond me that there's so much divisiveness today about everything—that family members don't speak to each other because one's a Republican and the other is a Democrat. Politics should never get in the way of a relationship.

Arthur was getting impatient because he had had enough of liv-ing in sin for two years and wanted us to get married, but when I referred to getting a divorce—or *trying* to get a divorce—as a job, I wasn't kidding. Finding Ed was still a full-time pursuit, espe-cially since he didn't want to be found. A critical step in starting divorce proceedings is serving papers, which is impossible without an address. I spent two years on a manhunt, tracking clues and fol-lowing every lead. I probably would have had better luck putting a message in a bottle and hurling it into the ocean. Arthur decided he would find me a lawyer who was sure to get the job done. When I went to his law office for our first meeting, he was sitting in front of a huge painting of a shark, and I thought, *Well, I've come to the right place.*

The manhunt ended when I found out that Ed had a lawyer in Canada. Once we had that piece of information, my divorce was finalized, and I was truly free. Arthur and I married in a civil ceremony at the apartment, surrounded by our children: Whitney, Stephen, Charles, Arthur Jr., Emily, and Serena. There was some disapproval on Arthur's side, as there often is when a father marries a younger woman. I think one of his daughters may have even tried to persuade him to back out while we were waiting for the judge to arrive. But Arthur was resolute, and fortunately, the judge was punctual, so it all worked out.

Marriage is always a leap of faith with an uncertain outcome; witness my two previous attempts. But I'm an optimist, so my motto is "Eat, drink, and remarry." Never stop believing that this time will be different. In my case, the third time was the charm. Arthur and I came to each other late in life, which made us even more determined to enjoy the time we had together.

Ask Me Anything:

Entertaining

How do you decide where to seat guests at a dinner?
When I plan a dinner, I like to add variety by inviting guests who have different professions and interests. I usually put someone who's talkative next to someone quiet, and I always separate couples because I don't want them to talk to each other all night.

Some of the dinners on Southern Charm *get a little heated, and guests often misbehave. How do you handle unruly guests?*
I don't have unruly friends, and my guests never fight at the dinner table! It's only on *Southern Charm* that you'll see behavior like that.

What is the appropriate reaction when a guest spills a drink (hopefully not red wine!) or breaks something at a party?
The trick is *not* to have a reaction. You simply accept it, smile, and try not to make the person feel embarrassed or uncomfortable. If it's broken, just whisk it away and deal with it the next day.

Do you play music when you entertain, and if so, what's on your playlist?
I don't usually play music because I think it interferes with conversation.

Is there a polite way to let guests know a party is over?
As the party is winding down, I walk around the room and start extinguishing the candles. If it gets really late and the stragglers haven't taken the hint, I collect glasses, even if someone is mid-drink. I wouldn't be afraid to shut it all down by dimming the lights, but it rarely comes to that.

Do you have a favorite hostess gift?
I like to bring an orchid or a box of candy. I never bring fresh flowers because it means the hostess has to find a vase and fill it with water, and that's inconvenient. And I don't bring wine because my taste may not be their taste. Now, of course, you should bring this book!

Ten

A fter we married, Arthur decided to sell Overbrook Farm, which was old, oversize, and more like a country club past its prime than a home. We weren't looking for a house to replace it, but one day, Arthur and I were driving on the Long Island Expressway and decided to get off the highway at Oyster Bay to do a little exploring. We found ourselves on a private road that led to Centre Island. It wasn't really an island but an isthmus shaped like a fishhook, formed by glaciers and once owned by the Matinecock tribe, who used it as a seasonal retreat, like the Hamptons. Dutch settlers who found their way there in 1639 reported seeing oysters "a foot long and broad in proportion" and described it as a Garden of Eden.

Guards were stationed at the road's entrance, but we explained that we just wanted to look at the houses, and they let us through. Then, we spotted a gate with a "For Sale" sign. Fate had led us to Southerly, a jewel of a Greek Revival house with graceful columns set on a magnificent sweep of acreage surrounded by white beaches and the bluest water.

When I got home that night, I called my friend Deeda Blair to see if she knew anything about it. Let's talk about Deeda. People are understandably dazzled by her appearance: she wears—no, *inhabits*—couture ensembles as if they're her second skin and has long been a fashion icon. In 1961, she married William McCormick Blair, President John F. Kennedy's ambassador to Denmark. Subsequently, Lyndon Johnson appointed Blair US ambassador to the Philippines. In diplomatic circles (and everywhere else in society), Deeda was celebrated as a skilled hostess with a formidable sense of style. But that wasn't enough for her.

She forged a relationship with Mary Lasker, a philanthropist who was best known for leading the War on Cancer, and public health became Deeda's mission in life. Deeda was boots-on-the-ground in research laboratories and hospitals, immersing herself in the science of the causes she supported. She was appointed vice president of the Albert and Mary Lasker Foundation, served on the board of the American Cancer Society, and when the AIDS crisis began, she was on the front line, formulating an emergency response, raising money, and working with researchers to achieve rapid breakthroughs.

Her knowledge, the result of hard work, was so vast that she could hold her own with any scientist. She was called a "rainmaker," an "idea factory," and a "matchmaker" because she had a gift for connecting people from various worlds—entrepreneurs, thought leaders, and great medical minds—who became stronger and more effective when they worked together.

In addition to her impressive résumé, Deeda is also a great friend and mentor who can be counted on for goodwill and good advice. I first met her when I lived in Washington, then we both moved to New York and saw each other frequently.

When I asked her if she knew anything about Southerly, she

knew *everything*. She told me it was owned by the Ansari family, relatives of the shah of Iran, and she had been there.

"It's a fabulous house," she said, and she was certain I would love it.

I called the agent immediately, and Arthur and I drove out to see it; it was love at first sight. We bought Southerly without looking at any other property.

My next call was to Mario, telling him that Southerly was a blank canvas. This time, he had free rein to work his magic. Let me be clear that it was a formidable challenge because he had to blend Arthur's pieces from Overbrook Farm with my antique furniture, mostly inherited from my mother, and my collections of Delftware, silhouettes, and dog art, to name just a few of my obsessions. Luckily, Mario had a lively sense of humor and a broad streak of whimsy. He thought a painting of a pug enhanced a room.

It was a big house, so of course we had to go on shopping sprees, which usually meant visiting antiques shops in Paris or London, where we could find authentic English country antiques. Mario taught me so much about the right way to create a room, and it is never about buying a container of high-priced furniture and dropping it into the space. When Mario began a project, he liked to spend at least a weekend in the home to see how the rooms succeeded, failed, or could be improved. He might add cornices, baseboards, or change everything, and these fundamental elements had to be in place before he even thought about moving forward with color and other design choices.

The expression "like watching paint dry" best describes Mario's process. While choosing a paint color or a wallpaper, he first had to see the room in every light, natural and artificial, so it could take days, weeks, or *months* for him to decide.

Ironically, it was love at first sight for me when I went to Zuber & Cie to select wallpaper for the dining room at Southerly. The company was founded by Jean Zuber in France in the nineteenth century. His wallpaper panels were considered works of art, prompting King Louis-Philippe to award him the Legion of Honor in 1834.

My parents had Zuber wallpaper in our dining room in Richmond. Titled "Scenic America," the paper depicted images of ladies in their beautiful dresses along with their carriages and horses. The entire series, which shows life in Boston, Niagara Falls, New York Harbor, and other quintessentially American places, is on display in the Diplomatic Reception Room at the White House.

I was studying my family's genealogy while I was putting the finishing touches on Southerly and had just learned of the role my ancestors played in the Revolutionary War. At Zuber & Cie, I was drawn to a wallpaper series called "The American War of Independence," which was printed in 1835. When I looked at its beautifully rendered scenes of the American Revolution, I felt my personal history come to life and had to have it.

Installing the paper was difficult. The walls had to be prepared in a certain way with a specific material and backing that would allow it to be removed if I ever relocated. I considered it a work of art and would always find a place for it wherever I lived. After the hanging was complete, we brought in Prudence Carter, a trompe l'oeil artist, to do some retouching. She painted a small image of Sally, our twenty-year-old cat who had been with Arthur since she was a baby, in the background, which I thought was a lovely sentimental touch.

Mario finally reached the point when he was ready to select and orchestrate the furniture. He was judicious in his choices and mindful of scale. Before I met Mario, I always wondered why the chair or sofa I fell in love with at the store looked so wrong when I brought it home. The problem was scale. I didn't pay attention to the size of the piece relative to the room or the other pieces of furniture. A low chair looks better near a high bookcase. It's a dance to get it right, and Mario knew instinctively what worked.

He also considered the floors and thought about when to use a rug and when to bring in an artist to paint a design. And what about the ceilings? A subtle shift in color, barely discernable and something no one would ever notice, could change the entire look of a room.

I could go on about Mario's incredible eye for detail and his many talents. But what I loved most about him was his big personality. He was the best companion—outrageous, irreverent, and fun! I think this story says it all. I brought him to an event at Buckingham Palace hosted by Prince Charles and Camilla. When Mario saw the couple coming over to greet us, he whipped out his favorite party trick, a rubber cockroach he'd named Harold, and set it down where they were sure to see it.

"If you're going to live in a palace," he scolded the prince cheekily as he pointed to Harold, "you could at least keep it clean."

Camilla, who had known Mario when she worked at Colefax and Fowler, a British company renowned for its fabrics and wallpapers, was well-acquainted with his pranks. "Jesus Christ, Mario," she said, with her throaty laugh. "Are you still doing that same old roach trick?"

Yes, he was, and it delighted him to no end. Later, he introduced new and improved versions of Harold, one on a string that he could pull around, and the pièce de résistance, a battery-operated cockroach that could move on its own. We were dining at a Mexican restaurant one night when Mario unleashed Harold and sent him scurrying across the bar. Everyone screamed and backed away . . . until Mario held up Harold and let them in on the joke.

I never knew what he would do next—show up in a wig and oversize gag glasses, use a fake accent on a prank call, or stage a pratfall on a flight of stairs in an antiques shop to terrify the owner. He even managed to turn serious occasions into comic moments. Mario often gave lectures, and one time, at a fancy seated luncheon, he spoke about "bringing the outside in," or incorporating nature in a room. While he spoke, he dumped an entire box of leaves onto the audience. Of course I was sitting right underneath him and was covered with more nature than I ever wanted to experience. He was Puck on steroids, which made life with Mario *very* interesting.

One of his favorite activities was seeing Dame Edna, the stage persona of Australian comedian Barry Humphries. I think Mario saw her show about forty-five times, and I accompanied him to at least ten performances. He couldn't get enough of her lavender wigs and outrageous humor. Whitney used to joke that Mario was "the Dame Edna of Decorators" because he was just as wildly entertaining.

While Mario worked on the interior of Southerly, we searched for someone to reimagine the landscaping. Deeda suggested that we hire Madison Cox, a garden designer who worked all over the world creating enchanting outdoor spaces for clients such as Marella Agnelli and Anne Bass. He designed the legendary gardens at Yves St. Laurent's Villa Mabrouka in Morocco.

Madison had a gift for enhancing natural beauty without making it look too tame or fussy. Mother Nature was his muse when he planted a rose garden in the back, built a little folly with a white fence around it, and added boxwoods and fruit trees. Inexplicably, Southerly's pool had a chain-link fence around it, which gave it the ambiance of a kennel. Madison replaced that eyesore with mature bushes that looked as if they had been there all along.

One of the most difficult projects was renovating Southerly's run-down dock. Obtaining a construction permit from the town officials was like renegotiating the SALT treaty. It took two years to win their approval, and only then could the work begin.

Thanks to Mario and Madison (who got on like a house on fire), Southerly was the showplace it was meant to be—everyone's favorite place in the summer, when we always had a full house. I invited my prettiest and most amusing girlfriends because they made Arthur smile. Taking full advantage of our waterside location, I bought a twenty-foot Boston Whaler and entertained our friends with cocktail cruises on Long Island Sound.

Rupert and Wendi Murdoch, our neighbors on Centre Island, were our guests on one of these excursions, and my little boat brought out Rupert's competitive side.

"Well, that settles it," he said. "I'm getting a three-hundred-foot boat!"

Was it a compliment because the boat was so much fun, or an insult because it was too small? With Rupert, you could never be sure!

Eleven

Arthur loved to travel, especially on trips involving art. He frequently loaned paintings to exhibitions at the Louvre and other international museums, and we would attend the openings in Milan, Japan, and equally far-off places wherever and whenever they were. We regularly made the rounds of art dealers in Paris and London, but one of our favorite destinations was Brittany. The wild, coastal landscape and dramatic light had inspired many Post-Impressionist painters, including Paul Gauguin. Amazingly, it was still possible to find their work there, so we embarked on treasure hunts two or three times a year.

I always felt most at home in London, where I had (and have) many friends. I spent a lot of time there when I was an art adviser, dashing around town; visiting dealers, auction houses, and museums; and I loved the city for its old-world gentility.

On one trip we made in the early nineties, Arthur and I attended a dinner hosted by Prince Charles at Clarence House, which was the residence of the Queen Mother at the time. On another occasion, a formal dinner at Buckingham Palace, with a blinding amount of royal silver on the table. Other invitations followed, and I never declined because these events enabled me to see paintings, all manner of antiques, and historic furniture from the Queen's vast collection of treasures.

The first time I met Prince Charles, he asked me where I was from. When I answered Richmond, Virginia, he told me that he had visited the plantations in Jamestown and the surrounding areas to study their architecture, preservation, and restoration. At our next encounter, we discussed art—I own a study of a painting of Queen Victoria's favorite pets, and Queen Elizabeth had the original in her collection.

I attended quite a few royal events over the years, and whenever I saw Prince Charles, now King Charles, I was impressed by his vision for England. He studied the past and understood the importance of preservation, but he also looked ahead for new ways to protect the environment.

The royals are also incredibly hardworking, notably Princess Anne, who attends multiple events in a day. These events are more likely to be held at a factory than someplace glamorous, and I credit her for being so dedicated. The royals raise money and awareness for charities and preserve great art, architecture, and decorative works. I'm not someone who's dazzled by the who-what-wear aspects of the British nobility. I'm an Anglophile and a royalist because I think the royal family has an incredible work ethic.

(Recently, I was invited to work with the Queen's Commonwealth Trust, the only charitable institution Queen Elizabeth founded herself, to identify fifty Americans to join the organization and participate in its philanthropic pursuits.)

After I married Arthur, I experienced another rarified world when I started going to the couture shows in Paris and did so for about ten years. You had to be invited to attend—the director of the fashion house reached out to learn when I would be arriving in Paris and the name of my hotel. Then, a special envoy delivered the sealed invitations (sealed because they were so coveted)—along with flowers, French candy, and maybe a little gift—to my hotel room.

One year, my friend Katie Lee told me that she would love to attend a show, so I arranged for her and her then husband, Billy Joel, to come with me to Chanel, which was always an extraordinary experience. We sat in the front row with Deeda Blair and then went to the Garden Room at the Ritz for lunch. Billy wasn't the only rock star in the room that day. Elton John came bouncing over to our table. He couldn't believe that Billy had just come from a fashion show, and he was even more incredulous that Billy was with *us*.

"You look so *demure*," he said, and I don't think it was a compliment, but it was funny. Somehow, two middle-aged ladies dressed in Chanel didn't fit his image of proper mates for Billy Joel.

Selecting a design from the runway during the shows was just the beginning of the process. I always saw more than I could afford and usually limited myself to two purchases—maybe a ball gown and a pantsuit with a silk blouse. Each garment was custom-made and required at least two to three fittings. Then, the fitters would come to New York with the semi-finished garments to refit them. There were fitters who specialized in ball gowns, others who did blouses and trousers, and even ones who concentrated on shoulders and wrists. The focus on detail was astonishing.

I always thought I was thin, but according to one fitter I overheard, a part of my anatomy was a problem. I understood just enough French to get the message loud and clear when she told her coworker—in rapid French—that it was a shame I didn't have smaller boobs because the fit would be more elegant if I were less endowed. Apparently, the French consider big boobs déclassé, but I never saw them as a problem.

I don't buy trendy clothes. I'd rather add one really good piece to my wardrobe and wear it forever, so I consider couture a good investment. But I'm also a collector at heart, and I view couture as an art form with all the attributes of a fine painting—the unique vision of the designer, the precious materials that bring it to life, and the artistry in every stitch and seam. A designer's atelier produces masterpieces rendered in fabric every day.

On a more frivolous note, the shows were fun! The music, the buzz of anticipation, then the dimming of the lights and the show itself—it was pure theater and exciting to be in the room. Haute Couture Week in Paris proved that there was still beauty and glamour in a world that would later embrace athleisure wear as an acceptable form of dress.

One show stands out in my memory: Balmain, 2001. Oscar de la Renta took over as creative director at Balmain in 1992 and designed the label's haute couture collections. I was a longtime fan of Oscar's work and became friends with him and Boaz Mazor, who ran his company in New York.

Boaz was handsome, one of the best-looking men ever, charming (the proverbial "sell-ice-cubes-to-an-Eskimo" charming), and a favorite guest at Southerly. He often came with his pet parrot and everything the bird might need—food, a cage, and even a blanket. The parrot was beautiful and better behaved than most of my guests. Boaz was inconsolable when the parrot died.

One time, when I visited Oscar and Boaz at their studio in New York, I was asked to wait outside. "Mr. de la Renta is with an important client," I was told. Usually, *I* was considered an important client and invited in immediately to have a cocktail and try on clothes. *Hmmm*, I thought to myself, *why am I out here in Siberia?*

I waited for about half an hour, then out came Nancy Reagan, the reason for the delay.

Boaz greeted me with a peace offering, a floor-length coat adorned with semiprecious stones. "It's the only one here in the United States," he promised, although he had made another for Princess Firyal of Jordan. Better still, he said he would charge me half price if they didn't have to put in the lining. I said, "Fabulous, I'll take it!"

As I was getting ready to leave, one of Boaz's assistants stopped me and asked if I would mind waiting so they could escort me out the back door. *Again!* Who was coming in? Hillary Clinton, that's who. Boaz had scheduled the former First Lady and the current First Lady with only half an hour between their appointments. That's cutting it close. I felt as if I were in a French farce. But it was bound to happen because Oscar dressed everybody.

And everybody planned to attend Oscar's Spring/Summer show in Paris on January 23, 2001.

Two days earlier, in Los Angeles, actress Renée Zellweger had won the Golden Globe for her performance in the film *Nurse Betty*. It was a funny moment when Hugh Grant announced her name from the stage because Renée was nowhere to be found. "Where is she?" he asked, "She's under the table? Renée is drunk, ladies and gentlemen. . . ." No, she was in the ladies' room, and millions of viewers watched as she ran to collect her award. She was so flustered and so blushingly girlish that the audience found her blooper charming.

Renée's upcoming movie, *Bridget Jones's Diary*, was poised to be a blockbuster. Anna Wintour, who always had her finger on the pulse of everything, planned to feature her on *Vogue*'s cover with an accompanying article chronicling the young star's adventures at the couture shows in Paris. Renée would be one of the first celebrities to sit in the front row at a couture show. Today, that row is filled with stars of questionable magnitude, influencers, and TikTok personalities. But at the time, the golden age of couture, was reserved for fashion heavyweights and clients who might actually *buy* the clothes. People cared about the process, not about being seen.

At Oscar's Balmain show, he entrusted Deeda Blair and me with Renée, who sat between us. Instead of paying homage to the designer by wearing one of his creations, Renée broke tradition by appearing in a gorgeous cream-colored suit, fresh from the Chanel runway that morning. There was a connection, Anna Wintour pointed out, demonstrating her encyclopedic knowledge of all things fashion. When Karl Lagerfeld, the creative director of Chanel, started out in the 1950s, one of his first jobs was working for Pierre Balmain.

The press was thrilled to see a young, radiant movie star in the audience of familiar couture veterans—new blood!—and the cameras never stopped flashing. "Stardust . . . is drifting around her like smoke . . . ," *Vogue* enthused, "Nikons blazing like Uzis." Arthur Elgort, a great American photographer on assignment for *Vogue*, took a picture of the three of us to capture the groundbreaking moment. After that, celebrities became a mainstay at the shows.

Deeda and I had a lovely time with Renée. Of course we did. She's Southern, meaning polite, charming, and easy to talk to. She was building a house in Los Angeles, so we had a spirited conversation about architecture and then whispered about our favorite looks as the models walked the runway.

Another person who I absolutely loved and couldn't get enough of in New York and Paris was Nan Kempner. Nan was thinner than anybody, *ever*—so thin that people speculated she was the inspiration for Tom Wolfe's memorable expression "social X-ray." The *New York Times* described her as being "as slim as a stalk of celery." But Nan actually had quite an appetite. Whenever we went out to lunch, she'd finish all her food and then take something off everyone else's plate.

The upside of being the thinnest woman in our circle (we were thin, but not *that* thin) and having a body like a hanger was that she could fit into the smallest size. When we went to Paris for the couture shows, she grabbed all the samples, a real coup because they were half-price. She amassed one of the most extensive collections of couture in the country. She was also a trendsetter, one of the first women to wear an Yves Saint Laurent pantsuit in the sixties. Her bold move met with resistance at the famed restaurant La Côte Basque, where she was denied admittance. But Nan solved the problem by taking off her pants, trusting that her tunic would keep her somewhat covered. "I didn't dare bend over," she said.

Diana Vreeland, the former editor of *Vogue*, a special consultant to the Costume Institute at the Metropolitan Museum of Art, and a legendary figure in the fashion world, said, "There are no chic women in America. The only exception is Nan Kempner."

Like many social icons, there was much more to Nan than met the eye. She was a serious student of fashion and knew the history of the clothes she wore. She taught classes in couture at the Metropolitan Museum of Art and was a contributing editor for French *Vogue* and *Harper's Bazaar*. She was also a design consultant for Tiffany & Co. Nan wore her expertise lightly, flippantly claiming she just loved to shop. She said, "I tell people all the time I want to be buried naked. I know there will be a store where I'm going."

In addition to being a famous clotheshorse, Nan was a celebrated hostess and a powerhouse philanthropist, raising more than $75 million for Memorial Sloan Kettering Cancer Center and piles of money for other charities.

It always amuses me when people assume that fashionable women who have made their mark in society are vacuous. Deeda and Nan could do anything—run a corporation, run the world— and should never be underestimated simply because they had great style. How they looked (and the beautiful clothes they wore) was the frosting on the cake. Although having style is an accomplishment, too.

To highlight a few of my remarkable friends, Georgette Mosbacher is another example. We met at a party in the early nineties and bonded immediately. Georgette, who grew up in Indiana, and I had a lot in common, including an Annie Oakley ability to handle a firearm. She had just come back from a pheasant-shooting trip, and I told her stories about going to Ireland with my father to shoot.

If you ever want to clear a room in New York, talk about your favorite guns.

She's been called "Hurricane Georgette," and it's an apt description. Georgette is a lifelong entrepreneur who has been the CEO of international corporations, including La Prairie; a political activist; a philanthropist; a successful writer; and, most recently, a diplomat when she served as the US ambassador to Poland. She can raise huge amounts of money for a cause with one phone call, deconstruct the most complicated political treatise, and swipe on red lipstick with equal skill.

Georgette wasn't born to wealth and power—she was a self-made woman who worked tirelessly to fulfill her many ambitions. Anyone who has read her books, *Feminine Force: Release the Power Within to Create the Life You Deserve* and *It Takes Money, Honey: The Smart Woman's Guide to Creating Total Financial Freedom* knows that she is brilliant and fearless. We can all learn from her.

And speaking about strong women, can we talk about Joan Rivers? We met at a dinner party hosted by Georgette. The other guests quickly became background noise because Joan, who was seated next to me, kept me laughing the entire evening. We became friends, and Mario and I regularly went to dingy little New York comedy clubs in unfamiliar neighborhoods to listen to her try out new material.

I also saw her at Buckingham Palace, of all places. The royals loved her, probably because she was so irreverent. Joan would say *anything*. We had a funny experience at a cocktail reception at the palace. We ran into Marylou Whitney in the ladies' room and let's just say that she had been overserved at the party.

Poor Marylou was so tipsy that she couldn't pull up her panty hose. Joan and I looked at each other, resigned. It was a nasty job, but somebody had to do it. Joan took one side, and I took the other. We yanked, tugged, and pulled until we somehow managed to solve Marylou's problem, an amazing accomplishment because we were weak with laughter the whole time.

My friend Renvy Pittman is another example. Renvy was working at a small recruiting company when data centers were being built in Dallas–Fort Worth, and there was a need for specialized software developers and programmers. Renvy, one of the few women working in technology at the time, made it her mission to master the basics of mainframe computing and opened her own recruiting company. Subsequently, she pivoted to careers in decorating and jewelry and achieved great success through her own business acumen. She has contributed millions of dollars to philanthropic causes, including education, and lives in what I consider to be the biggest and most beautiful house in Hollywood. Whatever she does, she always does it well.

When I think about the extraordinary women who have been my friends, I want to hold them up as examples to the young women I meet today. Deeda, Nan, Georgette, Joan, Renvy, and I'll add my name to this list, came of age before feminism was a mainstream idea. Yet we had ambitions that exceeded the conventional expectations for women and set out to make something of our lives.

I also have young friends who are ambitious and accomplished. Emily Selter is an art historian and writer. Luzanne Otte graduated from Yale and Notre Dame Law School and worked in the office of the general counsel for the Archdiocese of Los Angeles and at a major Los Angeles commercial real estate firm. They're smart, sophisticated, and serious about their futures.

My advice to young women is that they should stop worrying about meeting the right partner and concentrate on finding themselves. They should be concerned with establishing a career, focusing on their education, and having lives that make them interesting. They should be informed about what's going on in the world, develop opinions, and be involved in activities that enhance them and enhance their standing in the world. First and foremost, they should invest in *themselves*, have dreams, and work to achieve them.

That, by the way, is how you attract someone who is, shall we say, on your level!

Twelve

———— ✦ ————

My trips to Paris to attend the couture shows resulted in more than a fabulous wardrobe: I also met my dear friend André Leon Talley. He was the most charming, brilliant, and discerning man ever, which may be an understatement. At six foot six, he was a towering presence, literally larger than life—a man with a flamboyant sense of style, a stunning knowledge of subjects high and low, a great sense of humor, and deep faith.

His many accomplishments were all the more impressive given his humble beginnings. He was raised in Durham, North Carolina, by his doting grandmother, who supported him by working as a cleaning woman in a men's dormitory at Duke University. She encouraged his every ambition and watched proudly as he won a scholarship to Brown University and apprenticed with Diana Vreeland at the Metropolitan Museum of Art.

Identified as a rising talent, André worked at Andy Warhol's *Interview* magazine, *Women's Wear Daily*, and *Vogue*, where he started out as the fashion news director and ultimately became the first African American male creative director. My friend Cathy Horyn, a fashion critic and journalist at the *New York Times*, introduced us during one of my trips to Paris, and the fireworks between me and André started at a dinner.

I wore my favorite Yves Saint Laurent Le Smoking tuxedo coat-dress and carried a black evening bag. My outfit was on point, but what really captured André's attention was what he spied *inside* my demure purse. A bubble-gum-pink pistol. Locked and loaded. Don't ask why it was there. I think I had a fear of ending up alone on a dark street in Paris and wanted to protect myself just in case. And I knew how to use it.

Apparently, the sight of that fancy firearm signaled to André that there might be more to me than he thought. He wrote about the evening in his book *Little Black Dress*: "When I met Mrs. Patricia Altschul for the first time at a black-tie dinner in Paris, she wore this dress, and when she opened her elegant black envelope evening bag, I noticed she had a small pistol inside. How did she get a gun through customs? It was before today's strict laws." That pistol *really* made an impression.

Once we started talking, there was no stopping us, and our long-standing friendship evolved over cocktails and dinners in New York. André would take me to La Grenouille, the legendary French restaurant known for its classic cuisine and extraordinary floral arrangements. One night, he hosted a dinner in the private room upstairs. He invited the most interesting friends, including Mariah Carey and her manager, Benny Medina; Cornelia Guest; Mario; and two of my favorite writers—Julia Reed and Dominick Dunne.

Dominick and I hit it off that night and became great friends in that *you can tell me everything* way. Whenever we ran into each other at a party, we'd whisper, "Where are you sitting?" If we weren't seated next to each other, we'd "reorganize" by discreetly moving the place cards, which was totally improper, and we knew it. But we were unwilling to let rules stand in the way of a great evening. We'd put our heads together, and Dominick would survey the room and whisper stories about the other guests.

We also met for long, chatty dinners at Swifty's, the see-and-be-seen insider restaurant on the Upper East Side of New York that felt like a private club. Mario helped decorate the space, so I felt completely at home, especially in the back room, where the most coveted tables were tucked away. The menu wasn't fancy: the glitterati, literati, and society regulars came for the meat loaf and the burgers. Guests at private parties were treated to "millionaire's bacon," crispy strips of bacon coated with caramelized brown sugar—an hors d'oeuvres I still serve today.

My favorite dish at Swifty's was shad roe. I won't describe it in detail because it involves the egg sac of a female shad fish and sounds disgusting, but it was incredibly delicious and very hard to find on a menu.

It was a great place for people-watching, and Dominick knew everybody. He also knew all the latest gossip and where the bodies were buried. Eventually, some of his juicy stories would surface in his novels—I think he was trying out material on me, and I was his spellbound audience. As a social satirist, Dominick was ruthless in portraying the very rich at their very worst. In life, he was a sweet, kind, and generous man, and I loved being in his company.

I felt the same way about Julia Reed, who wrote spirited accounts of growing up in the South and chronicled culture, politics, food, and whatever caught her fancy in her books and in publications, including *Vogue* and *Garden & Gun*. Always irreverent, insightful, and entertaining, Julia could make any subject interesting.

The last time she visited me in Charleston, I hosted a party for her. Somehow, it came up that she knew John D. MacDonald's family. I told her that I used to play with Prentiss MacDonald in

Florida when I was a child and pulled out the faded black-and-white photographs to show her. She took them with her—maybe she was inspired to write about them—but she died a few months later, at the impossibly young age of fifty-nine.

I met many of André's friends over the years, and some became my friends. Of course I introduced André to Arthur, who adored him and always got a big kick out of the lively conversations we had when he visited. My husband and my friend may have seemed like an incongruous pair—Arthur was completely indifferent to fashion. I mean, he was still wearing things that he wore at Yale in 1941. But Arthur and André had so much in common. Both men could opine endlessly about any subject. And, both Arthur and André spoke French beautifully and were well-versed in French history and art. Arthur usually spirited him off to his library or art vault to show him transparencies of paintings he might acquire.

André would pop in for lunch frequently and visit us at Southerly. Whenever we went to an event at the Met and took a table, we would always bring André. When André spoke, Arthur was completely mesmerized. He loved that André never held back. André's opinions, like the man himself, were larger than life.

André never minced words, and I could always count on him to be absolutely frank with me about everything, like when we attended a luncheon together and I wore a Dolce & Gabbana dress with cats all over it. I loved the dress and thought it was lovely and whimsical, but after lunch, André pulled me aside and said, "I don't ever want to see you in that cat dress again!" Apparently, it mortally offended him. After that incident, it became a funny *cat*chphrase between us.

"Don't be wearing that cat dress," he'd warn whenever we made plans together. Only André could make an insult funny.

One night, we had plans to attend an event at the Met, which was right across the street from my apartment, and he came by to pick me up. The weather was warm, so I stepped out of the building wearing a chic black dress and high heels but no stockings. André took one look at me and squealed, "Fumé, fumé!" I had no idea what he was saying, but I knew it sounded bad.

"For God's sake," he said. "Put on some dark stockings!"

Apparently, my bare legs needed to be smoke-colored to complete the look. When André spoke, I listened. I raced upstairs to correct my faux pas because André always knew best.

Well, almost always. I had lunch with André at L'Avenue after an Yves Saint Laurent couture show in Paris. Everyone was watching the clock, waiting for the runway samples to come back to the showroom so we could dash over to try them on before Nan Kempner scooped up everything. As we were leaving the restaurant, it started to pour. I suggested that we make a run for it, but André looked horrified. He was decked out in a flashy red alligator coat by Prada, and he said, "If you think I'm going outside with this new alligator coat, you're crazy!"

Like a true Southerner, I considered alligators in the same genus as cockroaches. They're pests, and I reminded him they *live* in the water. What's going to happen if an alligator gets wet?

André had a famous habit of screaming, and he let out *that* scream in protest. Then, he took my hand and announced, "We're having coffee and dessert and waiting this out." We were there for two hours. By the time I got to the showroom, all the good samples had been snapped up—a maybe not-so-small price to pay for the pleasure of his company.

André found inspiration everywhere, even on Third Avenue at seven in the morning. On his way to an appointment, he spied a chair in the window of Scalamandré, the company famous for its beautiful textiles. The chair was upholstered in a fabric that depicted a Tuscan scene, with cockerels fighting on a vivid blue background.

His first thought? A ball gown: "A bold print for a summer ball or a special dance," he imagined. And he knew just the person who would be game enough to wear a gown made of interior decorating fabric and not worry about looking like a piece of furniture. Me! I suspect that he was thinking of Scarlett O'Hara, my style muse, when she famously turned her old parlor curtains into a dress.

André called me and said that I was "as Southern as Southern can get" and that Lars Nilsson and Hervé Pierre, the designers at Bill Blass, were willing to whip up "a hoopla" of a dress and a matching shawl. I immediately said yes because, as I explained to him, I've worn big ball gowns since I was a teenager.

I was always the tallest child, a head taller than all the boys who came to the tea dances and cotillions. As humiliating an experience as that was, I didn't hide or try to make myself look smaller. Instead, I wore ballerina-length, tulle, strapless dresses with big skirts. Nothing's changed, including my long hair, which André called my homage to Veronica Lake, the 1940s movie siren who covered half her face with a sultry peekaboo wave. She was before my time, so I thought it was *my* look, and it was inspired by a cowlick that annoyingly pushed my hair in that direction.

Fifteen yards of Scalamandré fabric and multiple fittings later, we had a photo shoot at Southerly. Wearing the spectacular ball gown that was so big it barely fit into my car when we transported it, I posed in front of a panel of the antique Zuber wallpaper in the dining room. André's instinct was correct. The dress was stunning.

"I love my big ball gowns," I confessed, as if it were a guilty pleasure. And my hope at the time (when I still attended balls) was that this old-fashioned "more is more" sensibility would come back. There was too much nudity in fashion, in my opinion. I anxiously awaited a new repressed era, something with a Victorian sensibility.

My grandfather
General Frank E. Dey.

My mother, Frances Pearl Sudler,
on one of her voyages.

My father, Dr. Walter
Pettus Dey, when he
graduated from Tulane
medical school in 1907.

The Dey Mansion in Wayne, New Jersey.

All photos are from the author's personal collection unless otherwise noted.

Always on a horse!

Hand in hand with my father.

Flirting with the camera at boarding school.

My friend Michael Maroney.

An art advisor at work.

Arthur, the love of my life.
(Photograph by Jonathan Becker)

A cocktail cruise on Oyster Bay.

Wedding at sea with Ed Fleming.

Young love and a cocktail . . .
with Lon.

Baby Whitney.

Whitney plotting his next adventure.

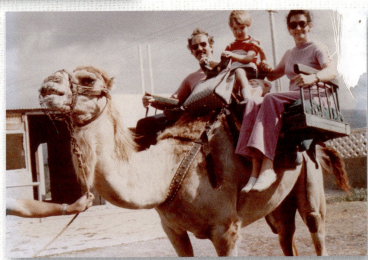

Family vacation,
Canary Islands.

Front row at Balmain with Deeda Blair and Renée Zellweger.
(Arthur Elgort/Condé Nast via Contour RA by Getty Images)

Dinner at Buckingham Palace with Prince Charles (now King Charles).

At the Met Gala with André Leon Talley. *(Steve Eichner/WWD/Penske Media via Getty Images)*

With Oscar de la Renta.

Who wore it better, me or Scarlett O'Hara?

(Photographed by Jonathan Becker)

Mario (Buatta) being Mario.

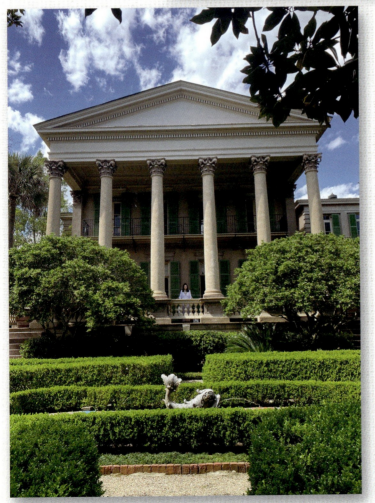

The Isaac Jenkins
Mikell house.

The dining room with its wonderful Zuber wallpaper . . . and Siegfried and Roy. *(Photo by John Neitzel)*

Mario Buatta at his best. *(Photo by Laurey Glenn)*

Thanks to Mario, my bedroom is a beautiful place to dream. *(Photography by Patrick Brickman / Charleston Home + Design Magazine)*

Whitney's first Ascot.

Whitney in LA.

#1 son! *(Courtesy of Bravo Media LLC)*

Lovely Lily.

Who let the dogs out?

Ambassador Georgette
Mosbacher and Guinevere.

Silhouette Queen.

With Renvy Pittman.

Madison LeCroy, your secrets are safe with me.

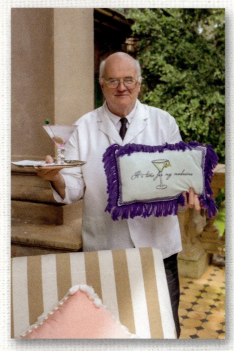

Michael could do anything, from serving a perfect cocktail to modeling for my HSN line.

I was born to be on a float— World Pride Day. *(Courtesy of Bravo Media, LLC)*

Michael coloring my hair during the pandemic.

Stormy weather. *(Photo by Rick Bhatia / From the author's personal collection)*

Watch What Happens Live with Andy Cohen. *(Courtesy of Bravo Media, LLC)*

Cheers from *Southern Charm.*
(Courtesy of Bravo Media, LLC)

André quipped that I was a victim of what he called arrested debutante development, one of his funny wordplays.

No one was as clever as André. Bon mots tripped off his tongue, and he loved inventing words or finding an original way to make his point. Once, when expressing horror about something, he coined the term *dreckfull*, defining it as the lowest point in the lowest ebb . . . "a total, total, total hot mess." Another time, on *America's Next Model*, or one of those other fashion competition shows, he complained that a design was "the height of decrepitude," a hyperbolic criticism that took displeasure to a new level.

André loved to communicate by fax and, later, with the advent of the internet, by email. His personality came through in every line. He wrote spontaneously with wit, humor, a little sugar, and a lot of spice. He was a great social observer who could link the antics of today's socialite to a misbehaving aristocrat in the seventeenth century.

André was an equal-opportunity social arbiter, and everyone was fair game for his praise or his condemnation. Tom Ford aptly described André's impassioned opinions. "When he was excited, he was excited. When he loved something, he loved it. When he hated something, he hated it. He was never boring." I've saved André's messages because they're so *André*, and so much fun to reread.

From: André Leon Talley <andreleontalley@gmail.com>
Date: Wed, 24 Oct 2007 21:11:49
To: pataltschul@optonline.net
Subject: Re: Greatest lunch of all times

Dear Pat
    So glad you were there. You always look fabulous. I want to talk you about the Court of Charles II and Barbara

Palmer, Duchess of Cleveland and her six bastards, sired by the king. Reading Lady Antonia Fraser's brilliant, but shrill, shrill book.

I had a fabulous time. I thought it was great. Each great person has his own style. Love Rachel for coping with her mogul record king husband. Joe Armstrong is a blast. Grace High-tower, a new friend, wed to a great, great actor Robert de Niro.

Oh, I was so light-headed and giddy after the lunch, I rushed to The Met, to see the Baroque Tapestry show. Now there is something to see. Some are just the most breathtak-ing masterpieces. The colors are so rich, saturated, almost modern. And then of course, I fantasized about the throne panel and roof. Some are almost erotic with those gallop-ing horses, and battlescenes. You would love it. I was going to ask you to come but I thought swaning around in those skinny minny mouse [sic] heels would be too, too much on those stone floors.

The Met is a fantastic museum.

This weekend, I am off to Philadelphia for a church gala with Alexis. We are driving down, swaning in all our finery to a black tie gala so they will just gasp and lean back.

There are some incredible new dresses at Prada, simple black. Sack-back dresses in crepe, delicious. You would look good in them. Alexis tried on one, black crepe with a bow that just sort of hugs the derriere, but not in a vulgar way. They also have it in gray wool. Sleeveless. Simple, not too expensive.

Tomorrow, I am getting the first Oracle of Delphi Award by the Fashion Group. I am wearing a red Tiepolo red domino couture by Valentino. It arrived today. Glorious and

Baroque. Sort of Cardinal Richielieu [*sic*] with a feel of a kaftan , a Russian kaftan coat of Potekim [*sic*] proportions. I will look great. Love the sound of the fabric. Tomorrow, I will rehearse all morning the accepantance [*sic*] speech.

I wish I was smart enough to have had a lover, a rich lover to buy me a baroque tapestry! Where would you hang it? The rooms were so big. The walls must have looked extraordinary.

I would hang one in an empty room.

Andre

Dear Pat

Would love to be able to go on December 3rd.

I think the only day I could do lunch is sometime like November 7, 8.

I do think December 3rd might work. Because I realized. I don't have to really travel until December 5th to London for one day.

So put me down for sure for December 3rd. I've never been to one of those and would love to go.

I went to bed at 9 p.m. which is why I am up at this most uncivilized hour. I also have to spruce up the mess before Nora comes in to clean up, once a week. The clothes are all over chaise lounges and get the luggage put back. etc. etc.

Tonight I get this Oracle of Delphi Award, so look for me on the Web tomorrow in my Valentino--Ptomekin [*sic*] domino in the richest red around.

I will definitely accept for December 3rd right now.

You should go down to Lily & Cie with me one day, That way you can take the dress back to her directly and look at her collection. Mica bought the greatest coats. She has great coats.

We could do that after the lunch with Wendy? Up to you.

I am putting December 3rd in my book The Met, right now.

Andre

Ask Me Anything:

Fashion

I love clothes, but I'm on a budget. What are the best investment pieces, and what bargains look good and get the job done?

I think the best investment pieces are good bags and shoes, and a bag doesn't have to be a Birkin. There are so many classic and elegant bags out there. For shoes, invest in Manolo Blahnik kitten heels and Chanel ballerina flats. They sometimes go on sale, and you can also track them at liveauctioneers.com, a site where you can get incredible pieces at great prices. If you want to invest in a good dress that will serve many purposes, look for a perfectly tailored A-line sleeveless dress that falls beneath the knee, preferably in classic neutrals—black, white, or brown. As for my favorite budget buy, I get my leggings at Amazon. They're great!

No one wears a caftan like you! Please share your styling tips for making a caftan look fabulous. Shoes? Jewelry? Hairstyle? And are there any affordable designers who make flattering ones?

Many of my caftans come from Oscar de la Renta, but I've found some in India and Morocco, and you can get fabulous caftans on eBay. The trick is to take them to the tailor if they're too voluminous and have them slenderized so you don't look like you're wearing a tent. Flat shoes look best unless the caftan is going to be evening wear—then you can dress it up with strappy, flamboyant heels. Accessorize with statement necklaces and dangly earrings, and if you have long hair, wear it down to complete the bohemian look.

Your jewelry is stunning, and I'm sure most of it is the real thing. Do you have any fun faux pieces? Are there designers or brands you recommend?
I have some jewelry from India that was not expensive. And I collect costume pieces designed by Lawrence Vrba, whose dangly earrings look wonderful with caftans.

How do you select the right purse for the right occasion?
Size is the key consideration. Great big bags look good with casual clothes, but at night, you should use a smaller bag, ideally a clutch.

Thirteen

A rthur wanted to go everywhere. If he had his way, we'd be out every night and at the proverbial opening of an envelope. I finally put my foot down and said that we had to curate our activities. I blamed it on myself, claiming that having my hair and makeup done, wearing a dress and high heels, and staying out until the wee hours, Monday through Thursday, was just too arduous. But the truth was that Arthur started to have mobility issues when he was in his late seventies, and I was concerned.

We were in London the first time I noticed. We hailed one of those old black taxis that are high up off the ground. Arthur had trouble climbing in—he just didn't have the strength to raise his legs—and I had to kind of pull him up into the taxi. From then on, we used a car service to take us to wherever we had to go. Then Arthur fell a couple of times, so we got him a cane. For whatever reason, his equilibrium was off.

But nothing could keep Arthur down, and he had a kindred spirit in Brooke Astor, the doyenne of New York society who ruled with an iron glove. She was a trustee at the Metropolitan Museum of Art, and we served on the chairman's council with her, so we saw her frequently. She was ninety-four when Arthur and I married, and whenever she came to the apartment for parties or to see Arthur's art collection, she always showed up in high heels, her power shoes.

I remember we ran into her at one event, and at this point, she was using a walker. Nevertheless, she was dressed to the nines and in full war paint. She sat beside Arthur, noticed his cane, and asked, "Isn't middle age distressing?" She was almost one hundred, so "middle age" was a bit of a stretch. But I loved her spirit. Like Arthur, she had the energy, determination, and joie de vivre of a much younger person. Brooke lived to the incredibly ripe old age of 105 and arranged for the words "I had a wonderful life" to be inscribed on her gravestone. She suffered from Alzheimer's disease during her final years, so she was spared the heartbreak when her son, Anthony Marshall, was accused of subjecting her to elder abuse and stealing from her estate.

Unfortunately, Arthur's deteriorating condition had nothing to do with "middle age." We consulted several doctors to determine why he was so unsteady on his feet, finally ending up at the Mayo Clinic, where they ran a battery of tests. The doctor asked him a million questions about his lifestyle, and Arthur tried to minimize his many indulgences.

"Do you drink," the doctor asked.

"Oh, a little bit," Arthur said.

"What do you mean by 'a little bit'?" the doctor pressed.

"Well, I always have a Scotch when I come home from Goldman Sachs."

I looked at him, and he clarified, "Well, maybe two, but they're weak. And sometimes we have wine with dinner."

"How often is sometimes?"

"Oh, well, I don't know. More often than not," Arthur dodged.

Now, the doctor was in full Sherlock Holmes mode. "I see," he said. "And what about smoking?"

I could tell Arthur was formulating an evasive answer, so I gave him another stern look.

"Oh, I forgot about that. Well, I do smoke cigars, and I usually have one with a brandy in the library. . . ."

He did enjoy himself, and I loved that about him. It was a sad day when Arthur was diagnosed with polymyalgia, an autoimmune disease that causes the musculature to degenerate. I pulled the doctor aside and asked, "What's going to happen? What's his life going to be like?" The news was not good. The doctor predicted a slow degeneration and gave him about two years to live. And that's exactly what happened. Arthur went from a cane to a walker to a wheelchair, at which point we had round-the-clock help—a male nurse for him during the day because Arthur was a big man and then a female nurse who would stay at night.

I did my best to give him the life he wanted, to keep him engaged and not miss any important events. We couldn't navigate stairs, so restaurants like 21 were out of the question. However, we discovered that many places had ramps and secret doors that led to more accommodating entrances. Arthur never let his wheelchair get in his way, and if he was game, *I* was game.

We still went to Southerly on weekends, and one of his favorite activities was going to the Seawanhaka Corinthian Yacht Club in Oyster Bay, one of the oldest yacht clubs in the western hemisphere, where they would shoot the cannon off to mark the end of the day and serve cocktails at six o'clock. Arthur loved to sit outside and look at the boats and the water. I wanted the house to be lively, so I always invited guests, the ones he found most engaging and fun. Arthur suffered physically, but he never, ever lost his keen intelligence, wonderful personality, or curiosity about everyone and everything. The party never ended.

We even made two trips to Europe on the Concorde with both nurses in tow. On one of the flights, we headed to Paris to visit an art dealer friend when the unthinkable happened. Arthur was sitting in front of me, and we had just been served breakfast when the Concorde blew an engine as it reached Mach 2. Suddenly, the plane shook like crazy, and cups and plates flew through the air. I looked out the window and realized I would soon be seeing water. We were going *down* instead of up!

Then, Arthur started pushing the help button. Immediately, I imagined the worst, thinking that the terrifying situation had provoked a heart attack.

I yelled, "Arthur, Arthur, are you all right?"

In his calmest voice, he answered, "I'm fine. My roll fell off my breakfast tray, and I'm ringing for an attendant to pick it up." That was Arthur—unperturbed when everyone else was panicking.

Seconds later, the plane leveled off and began to ascend. Death was averted, and Arthur got a fresh roll.

It wasn't until the last couple of months that he really failed, and I could see the end coming. One of our cats sensed it, too. Sweet Rocky, a beautiful Himalayan we had adopted together, was devoted to Arthur and refused to leave his bed.

Arthur died in his sleep on St. Patrick's Day, 2002, at the age of eighty-two. He was a remarkable man. I was so lucky to have been with him, even if it was just for twelve years. When we were together, we were really together, making each other so happy.

I was inconsolable and couldn't imagine a future without him.

Fourteen

I have nothing positive to say about being a widow.

With Arthur's passing, all the life and light had seemed to have left the house. Then, after Arthur's funeral, André came to Southerly for a long visit and dedicated himself to lifting my spirits. It was impossible to feel the weight of the silence with André in the room, and he eased me through my darkest hours by insisting that we wear caftans, binge on pizza, and watch movies. We settled into a comfortable routine. He was a wonderful distraction, and he didn't leave until he was sure I was on the right path.

I spent a year dismantling the New York apartment. And running an estate as large as Southerly was a full-time job. The household staff—a cook and two housekeepers—had to be supervised. The gardeners were there every single day. And then there were the unforeseen catastrophes—the new well that had to be dug; the roof that needed a fix; the list was endless. Worse still, my butler was leaving, and I had to replace him. It may sound like a high-class problem, but at Southerly, a butler's presence was a necessity.

Most people think of the butler as a tuxedo-clad man bearing a silver tray or the character in a game of Clue. The International Butler Academy (yes, there really is such a school) compares the modern butler to a Swiss Army Knife, specifying that they must be multitaskers who are knowledgeable, organized, efficient, and skilled at problem-solving. But I think the position is more elevated—in real life, a butler is the CEO of a domestic corporation, and a good one is very hard to find.

Mario told me that Mrs. Eleanor Bostwick, an ancient dowager who maintained an enormous estate in Old Westbury, New York, had passed away and that her butler would need a new position. "Move quickly," he warned, because prospective employers would descend on Michael Kelcourse in droves. Single women are famous for chasing widowers as soon as they become available, but the pursuit of a good butler is even more cutthroat.

I abandoned any sense of propriety and contacted him immediately—poor Mrs. Bostwick wasn't even cold. We met, and I liked everything about him. He had been classically trained by the ninety-year-old butler who attended Mrs. Bostwick before him in a household that employed eighteen domestics. He radiated competence, had very high standards, and beneath his composed—even detached—exterior, he had a dry wit and a killer sense of humor. He also loved animals, which was good because I always had a menagerie. I persuaded him to work for *me*, leaving my competition in the dust. Best decision I ever made. With Michael in place, I became "Mrs. A," and all was right with the world.

Gradually, I built a new life. The first step . . . finding an apartment in New York City. I turned to Alice Mason, the queen of New York real estate, to help me on this quest. Alice wasn't just a real estate broker—as the *New York Times* said, she was a social engineer. She knew about the best apartments before they were available, and, more important, she was a master at navigating the gatekeepers, the fussy and often capricious co-op board chieftains who delighted in finding reasons to turn away applicants.

Alice's advantage was her elevated social status. She hosted highly curated dinner parties for New York's richest and most powerful players, and guests could count on being in the company of one, maybe two US presidents. At one table, architect Philip Johnson and arts patron Agnes Gund. At another, writer Norman Mailer, publisher Malcolm Forbes, and producer Norman Lear. At one dinner, Claus von Bülow, who had recently been acquitted of trying to kill his wife, Sunny, snidely wondered (while he was feasting on Alice's food, I may add) why people would come to an event hosted by a *Realtor*.

He was told off by an indignant guest who said that everyone in attendance was famous for something. "And," the guest added, "you're here because you're a famous murderer."

Alice's invitations were never declined. Even the elite needed help securing the best address.

I had my heart set on a maisonette we found in one of *those* buildings—960 Fifth Avenue. The amenities included a catering facility headed by a French chef and staffed by waiters trained at Buckingham Palace, and a fabulous gym. Alice warned that I would be up against what she considered the toughest co-op board in the city. In her experience, they rarely approved any applicant. I already had one strike against me, she pointed out, because I was a single woman. Boards were leery of unattached women who might have questionable morals. Unattached men, of course, were fine.

She advised me to use my best connections to present stellar letters of recommendation—seven of them—and to offer $50,000 over the asking price. I assembled the Patricia Altschul bible, a dossier of every tax return and financial form imaginable and prepared to meet the firing squad—six somber men in suits. We met in the multimillion-dollar apartment owned by the chairman of the board.

Luckily, the real estate gods were with me that night. When I walked into the apartment, I noticed a painting above the fireplace. I released my inner art adviser and said, "How wonderful! You have a van de Velde. It's so beautifully painted. Is that an early work or a later one?"

I had the owner at hello. It's rare for a person to recognize a van de Velde, and my host was flattered that someone knew and appreciated his painting. His icy demeanor thawed, and he told me that it was actually Arthur who had convinced him to buy Post-Impressionist paintings when he first started collecting. We bonded over art that night, and I think that persuaded the board to approve the application of the Merry Widow. How loose could I be if I knew my way around Post-Impressionist paintings?

Once the apartment was secured, I called Mario to tell him it was time to get to work. He knew the space because the apartment originally belonged to Sister Parish, the famous interior designer. It changed hands after she died, and the new owner let it deteriorate into a dirty, dingy, and disgusting mess that needed new windows, new electrical and air-conditioning systems, a new kitchen and bath . . . new everything. Mario was confident that he could make it great again.

This time, I wanted a little sparkle. "Not over the top," I explained to *Architectural Digest* when the magazine featured a story about the renovation, "but lush, exotic—a glamorama."

Mario waved his magic wand and came up with silver-tea-papered walls for the living room that cast a subtle sheen. "You need a fireplace on this wall to focus it, and I'm going to do it whether you like it or not!" he announced when planning the rest of the room.

Fine, I thought, *but there is no fireplace. How is that going to happen?* Mario found an eighteenth-century mantel and built a *fake* fireplace, that's how. Problem solved. Fake or not, when it was finished, guests instinctively tried to sit close to it as if to warm their feet before the fire.

The draperies in my bedroom were a decorative tour de force. Mario created couture curtains—opulent panels of mauve, peach, and pink taffeta trimmed with glimmering crystals. And if I needed a gown for the Met Gala in a pinch, I could go full Scarlett O'Hara, pull these beauties off the wall, and wear them.

The dining room, carved from the apartment's spacious entryway, was a Moroccan fantasy, dark, with bamboo framing like a gazebo. In the kitchen, we preserved some of Sister Parish's touches, including cupboards painted with English rabbits, roosters, and a Pekingese serving tea. I can never resist vignettes of whimsical animals.

Fabulous things happen when you let Mario have his way and unleash his quirkiness. The apartment was a jewel box filled with treasure. I wanted sparkle, which is exactly what I got. Sparkly is fun, and I needed a little fun in my life as I forged ahead without Arthur.

The downside of living alone was that there were times when I couldn't close the zipper on the back of my dress, every single woman's nightmare. But the upside of living in my maisonette was that I could open my door and call out to the doormen, who were just steps away, and ask, "Can somebody zip me up?"

Now that's a full-service building!

Fifteen

———◦———

I eased back into the social life I had enjoyed with Arthur—dinners, gallery openings, and other art and fashion activities. A typical evening was the gala celebrating the Martha Graham Dance Company at the Plaza Hotel. All the usual suspects were there, including André, Mario, Oscar, Nan Kempner, and on Nan's arm, Kenneth J. Lane, the jeweler and perennial man-about-town.

Kenny's specialty was costume jewelry. He never worked with precious stones, yet everything he designed was distinctly Kenny Lane and sought after by women who possessed dazzling collections of the real thing. Jacqueline Kennedy Onassis, Audrey Hepburn, Princess Diana, and even Elizabeth Taylor, famous for wearing diamonds as big as the Ritz, flocked to Kenny for his signature pieces, which were bold, colorful, and dramatic.

Some women asked Kenny to make copies of their valuable jewelry. He received these requests frequently because, after he worked his magic, no one could tell the difference between the real piece and the imitation. He told me that when Jacqueline Kennedy Onassis decided to sell an evil eye pendant given to her by her husband,

Aristotle Onassis, she had him make a copy first—so she could have her cake and eat it too.

Kenny wasn't born into high society—in fact, he called *himself* a fabulous fake, but his talent and wit propelled him to the top of every insider list. He managed to be imperious and amusing at the same time. He wrote a memoir, which he titled *Faking It*, and when I teasingly asked him why I wasn't in it, he said, "Well, you know, you're lucky we're good friends because you don't have a title." That was Kenny, insulting, but *funny* insulting.

He gave me a present right after Arthur died—his version of an evil eye pendant, explaining that it offered protection against jealousy and ill will. "You're going to be needing this," he said cryptically.

"What do you mean?" I asked, wondering if he knew something I didn't.

"I can't go into it, but just wear it," he insisted.

Now I was really spooked. I didn't press him, but I wore it for years, afraid of the consequences if I dared to take it off. I guess it worked against whatever unknown threat was coming my way, but eventually, I put it in a drawer, and there it still sits.

A few months after Kenny gave me the pendant, Deeda and I attended a jewelry exhibition in London. Four hundred exquisite works by JAR, the jewelry designer Joel Arthur Rosenthal (who has been called "the Fabergé of our time"), were on display for the first time. JAR's creations were stunning (and stunningly expensive). His atelier in Paris was so exclusive that new clients couldn't pass through his Place Vendôme door unless they were recommended by other clients. If they were accepted, they were happy to pay any price for his masterpieces because they never lost their value.

To create an air of mystery, the JAR exhibition was staged to be unusually dark, so dark that visitors were given little flashlights to illuminate the jewels. Who did we see behind us in the dim light, furiously taking notes and snapping photographs? Kenny Lane, who was doubtless finding inspiration for his next fabulous fake.

But getting back to my story about the Martha Graham gala, Kenny Lane wasn't the only man in attendance whose name was synonymous with jewelry. Unbeknownst to the invited guests, a jewel thief was in our midst, a retired jewel thief, that is, who, during his thirty-year career, had stolen about $35 million worth of rocks. Bill Mason was a cat burglar extraordinaire who raided penthouses and palaces in New York, Palm Beach, and other tony places where the rich resided. Eventually, he packed up his tools, and when all statutes of limitations were safely behind him, he wrote a book about his crimes in high places, *Confessions of a Master Jewel Thief.*

He was at the gala with a *New York Times* writer who was curious about how a jewel thief would read the room. Was he dazzled by the "small glacier" of a twenty-caret diamond on Nan Kempner's right hand? Did he lust after the huge gold David Webb serpent coiled around the neck of the wife of Houston's former mayor? No. Mr. Mason was eyeing *me*.

He prided himself on his ability to identify a good mark, and he suspected I was flying under the radar by not wearing ostentatious jewelry. "Now, that's a woman who would interest me," he told the reporter. "She might not have much on her fingers, but I'll bet you anything she's got a lot more at home."

Well, he was right, but when I read the article in the *Times* the next day and saw that the reporter included my name, I was a little nervous and hoped the thought of my stash of jewels didn't coax this thief—or any other—out of retirement.

Of course, *the* gala was the annual one at the Met. Arthur and I started going in the early nineties. It was a totally different event back then, with a guest list consisting primarily of museum directors, art historians, curators, and collectors, not a crowd that would attract the attention of media outlets or the fashion police. By 2000, it had transformed into a Hollywood extravaganza with movie stars, rappers, and supermodels. As the guest list became more outrageous, so did the fashion.

André typically worked the red carpet, but in 2005, he decided to invite a date, and I was his lucky choice. André found the perfect dress for me at the Los Angeles vintage boutique LILY et Cie. It was one of Karl Lagerfeld's iconic Chanel ball gowns—a flurry of black organza and lace, voluminous and retro in all the right ways. That evening, André picked me up in a Maybach town car. The enormous skirt filled the back seat and blocked the rear window, and don't ask me how I got out of the car without a wardrobe malfunction. André was the best date—fabulous with a capital *F* and so much fun.

The next time I went to the gala, I wore a Balmain gown by Oscar de la Renta, a confection of black polka dots on a white background with a matching shawl lined in shocking pink.

Another year, I went with Mario (thankfully, he did not bring his cockroach, Harold, with him) and decorated my new Oscar de la Renta gown with a brooch I borrowed from Harry Winston. It must have been worth millions because the brooch came with two burly armed guards who followed me everywhere for the entire evening, lest I try to pull off a major jewel heist. A movie thief would have hatched an elaborate plan to switch the real brooch for a fake in the ladies' room, but I didn't have that kind of foresight and dutifully returned the loot at the end of the evening.

I was flattered when Anna Wintour picked out a gown for me to wear to the gala in 2008, until I saw that it was designed to fit a size zero model. A woman who loves fried chicken is never *that* thin. Vera Wang, the designer, had to make me a custom reproduction, which required five fittings! Whitney was my date that year, but he disappeared as soon we got inside, making a beeline for those size zero supermodels. I didn't see him again that evening.

Galas and nights out were fun, but my favorite evenings were the dinner parties I hosted at home, especially if Mario and Aileen Mehle were among the guests. Aileen was the social observer known as "Suzy," who penned a column for *Women's Wear Daily* and wrote for *Architectural Digest* and *W* magazine. She was called the "Grande Dame of Gossip," and had been reporting on the adventures (and misadventures) of high society for decades. She was so revered that she was the only gossip columnist invited to be a guest at Truman Capote's fabled Black and White Ball in 1966.

Most people couldn't wait to see their boldface name in her column, unlike Arthur, who was a very private person who never wanted to be mentioned. I didn't care about being in her column and had a more personal relationship with Aileen. The night she came over for dinner, she and Mario stayed after the other guests left, and we talked until two in the morning. Aileen had us howling at her no-holds-barred tales of life on the social circuit.

She traveled frequently to cover important parties and was often invited to be a guest at the homes of the rich and famous. Early in her career, she realized she was better off staying in a hotel than in their showplaces. In addition to being smart, witty, and a first-rate writer, Aileen was a very beautiful woman, so beautiful that she kindled the desire of one of her wealthy and entitled hosts.

She told us that she was dead asleep in Henry Ford's guest room when she felt someone pull back the covers and get into bed with her. Henry himself—uninvited and unwanted—came to claim her at 3:00 a.m., but Aileen managed to diffuse that uncomfortable situation and booked herself a hotel room for future trips rather than risk another run-in with a randy host.

I wish I could remember more of Aileen's war stories because they were sensational and much more entertaining than anything she could print.

Around this time, I set off on one of the most memorable—and extravagant—trips I've ever taken, thanks to my friendship with Baroness Hélène de Ludinghausen. Hélène is the last surviving member of the Stroganoff family who, beginning in the fourteenth century, amassed untold riches and a legendary art collection in old Russia. Hélène has a remarkable history. She was born in Paris during WWII, raised in Brazil, educated in Switzerland and Colorado, and returned to Paris to support herself as a shopgirl in a high-end boutique after her family suffered a financial reversal. There, behind the counter, she was discovered by Yves Saint Laurent, who saw that she was hardworking, sophisticated, and had an easy rapport with customers. He said, "I've found the lady who's going to run my house." His prediction was correct. At the age of twenty-eight, Hélène became the director of YSL, a position she held for thirty-one years.

Deeda introduced me to Hélène at YSL, and we became friends. Hélène knew everybody and hosted a legendary salon at her apartment in Paris that attracted the most interesting guests. The evening was always enlivened by the appearance of Hélène's pet pig, which had its own maid who followed it everywhere with a chamber pot, just in case.

Despite the fact that Hélène's family had been forced to leave Russia during the revolution, they instilled in her a deep love for her mother country. In 1985, she made her first pilgrimage there. She was saddened to see that the Soviet government had neglected the magnificent properties once owned by the Stroganoffs. Her philosophy was "Try to make everything pretty. Don't fall into the gloomies." So she tapped her connections to establish an international foundation to restore and preserve the homes, churches, and dachas that her family had built. To raise awareness and funds for her project, she organized trips to Russia, giving her guests unparalleled access to the country's hidden treasures.

I shared Hélène's passion for historic restoration and contributed to her foundation. When she invited me to come on one of her trips, I accepted immediately. We would spend a week visiting places handpicked by Hélène to show Russia at its best. There were so many events on the schedule, many of them formal, that I knew I needed help. I arranged for a dresser from Bergdorf Goodman to accompany me to take care of the multiple wardrobe changes every day, as well as my hair and makeup. Just to be safe, I shipped all my Yves Saint Laurent couture clothes to Paris, where I would pick them up right before our departure to Russia.

The best-laid plans . . . of course, my clothes didn't arrive on schedule. They were so late that I considered canceling my trip. Fortunately, they showed up at the very last minute, and I was able to go.

From the moment we arrived in Russia, the experience was magical. Our hotel was beautiful and luxurious, not what one might expect in the Soviet Union. The other people in the group were royals and luminaries, including Madame Bernadette Chirac, the wife of Jacques Chirac, the president of France, and the wife of Elie de Rothschild. Hélène had planned an extraordinary itinerary. We attended a special performance at the Bolshoi and a candlelit service at the cathedral in honor of Hélène and the Stroganoff family. The head curator at the Hermitage gave us a private tour of the museum's vaults, where I saw masterpieces I'd never seen in any art history journals. Rubens, Rembrandts—oh my God, so many Rembrandts—as well as works by Van Gogh, Monet, Michelangelo, and other artists.

Another high point was when Hélène took us to the insider place that had the best caviar I had ever eaten. We could buy as many tins as we wanted, but the catch was that we could take only two out of the country—which left me with one option: I stocked up, and every night for a week, when I got into bed, I ate an entire tin of caviar. It may be the most decadent thing I have ever done. I did it again at the airport when we were on our way home. I bought three tins and feasted on the extra one during the flight. Thanks to Hélène, I felt that I had experienced Russia the way the Stroganoffs did in more opulent times.

Meanwhile, back in the real world, André was having a problem. He always struggled with his weight—"I am just a sinner when it comes to food," he lamented. But he had gained so much weight that the people who cared about him worried he was endangering his health and staged an intervention. In 2005, Anna Wintour and a few trusted friends confronted André, urging him to go to a weight-loss clinic for a supervised diet. He was shocked by their appeal and refused to deal with it until a year later, when he seemed to have more insight into why he couldn't control his appetite.

A year after the intervention, he was ready to seek professional help at a clinic in Durham, North Carolina. Before he went, André called me with a request. He asked if I would be willing to accompany him to the clinic as his emotional support animal. It was the funniest and most touching invitation I'd ever received. The friend who pulled me from the black hole of grief needed my help, and I was happy to give it to him. I arranged to spend two weeks with him in Durham.

André picked me up at the airport wearing a Louis Vuitton fur stole over a tracksuit. He was an absolute vision. We checked into a hotel near the clinic at Duke University, where we reported for meals and exercise. We began the day with the mandated breakfast, took classes together, and then separated for sessions with our personal trainers. At the end of the day, we had a Spartan dinner and returned to the hotel. Sometimes, André gave me an article to read or shared a book he had to review, but mostly, we talked. André was a diva with hot and cold running emotions, so he had burned a few bridges in his time. Some he regretted, some not. The stories he told . . .

One night, we felt like going out, so he took me to a bowling alley in a predominately Black neighborhood. We walked in, and I looked around and said, "Gee, I feel a little out of place here."

"Now *you* know how it feels," he pointed out, and he was right. André never complained about experiencing racial prejudice or spoke of how difficult it had been for him to break through so many barriers, but I knew it hadn't been easy.

I worried about André's health, so I persuaded him to come to the Mayo Clinic when Whitney and I went for our annual checkups. At the airport, André showed up wearing an enormous pink tracksuit. All eyes were on him, especially when we went through security and the guards confiscated André's huge carry-on case. I had no idea what was in it, but they made us wait while they took it behind a curtain and examined the contents. I saw a man who looked like a mad scientist pull at least twenty bottles filled with various liquids from the case. They were unmarked, so each substance had to be tested.

"What in God's name is in those bottles?" I asked André.

He assured me he wasn't transporting the makings of an atomic bomb. They were his facial cleansers, he confessed. André had a very complicated skin regimen.

After a long, tense wait, his cosmetics were cleared, and we were on our way.

My best trips with André involved our fun-filled excursions to SCAD, the Savannah College of Art and Design. The college honored André with a Lifetime Achievement Award in 2001. From that moment on, he was the school's biggest champion and mentor in chief, making it a destination for the most important luminaries in the fashion world.

The award André received was renamed the André Leon Talley Award. With André's support and guidance, future recipients included Oscar de la Renta, Karl Lagerfeld, Miuccia Prada, Tom Ford, Ralph Rucci, and Diane Von Furstenberg, to name a few. The students were thrilled when these designers came to Savannah and engaged with them, sharing their stories and offering invaluable advice.

André and I ensured their visits to Savannah weren't all work and no play. We took them to the Olde Pink House, a historic restaurant housed in a 1771 mansion, where they dined on Southern classics: fried green tomatoes, fried chicken, fried *everything*, with sides of creamy grits and buttery corn bread. The meal alone was worth the trip.

But the city's star attraction was the grand empress of Savannah, the Lady Chablis. She was a famous drag queen who figured prominently in John Berendt's bestselling book, *Midnight in the Garden of Good and Evil*. When director Clint Eastwood set out to make a film based on the book, he planned to cast an actor in the role until he realized that no one could play Lady Chablis like Lady Chablis herself. She was fantastic and became one of the first transgender performers to be seen by a wide audience.

In Savannah, she frequently performed at Club One, and her sassy banter delighted our guests. I enjoyed her so much that I invited her to be the entertainment on an episode of *Southern Charm* when we celebrated Whitney's birthday. She was her usual outrageous self and took a fancy to Whitney. She fed him his birthday cake, scooping the icing up with her finger and sticking it in his mouth. He hasn't recuperated yet.

In addition to bringing so many incredible designers to SCAD, André established a costume collection as a resource for the students. He sourced museum-quality garments from Anna Wintour, fashion icon C. Z. Guest (donated by her daughter, Cornelia Guest), Elizabeth ("Lally") Graham Weymouth, Deeda Blair, and others, and in 2009, he convinced me to donate a sizable part of my couture collection, promising my treasures would have a good home.

I was a little nostalgic when I said goodbye to the classics and showstoppers that had been an important part of my wardrobe. They represented the fun times I had experienced in Paris with my friends and reminded me of the balls and parties I attended with Arthur on my arm. I felt that I was parting with a scrapbook of significant moments in my life. So many memories were woven in those seams. But I didn't dress like that anymore—these days, few events require a ball gown—and I was happy the students would be able to learn from them. And if I ever need a spectacular gown to wear, I know where they are.

My trips to Savannah confirmed what I had been thinking for a while: I missed the South—the food, the people, and the climate. Maybe it was time to go home.

Decor and Housekeeping Edition

Do you have any advice for someone who is nervous about buying a sofa? What would Mario say?

Mario would say, "I found you the perfect sofa for thirty-five thousand dollars!" But I have a better idea. Go to stairgalleries.com, where you can find a well-crafted, down-filled sofa that once cost somebody $35,000 and is now the price of an inferior sofa at a furniture store. You can buy your own fabric, have it recovered, and end up with an incredible sofa, much better than if you paid thousands of dollars for a new one.

You're accustomed to having household staff. What's the best way to have pleasant and productive relationships with people who work in your home?

First, *politeness* and *appreciation* are the two most important words. Hire people who are competent, dedicated, and dependable, and always treat them with respect. Anyone working in my house is a professional—someone who knows how to do the job. But if I have a particular way of doing something, I suggest (never order) that this has been a successful way I've done it in the past and offer details. Or, if something is precious, I take care of it myself. I use a special sable brush to clean certain picture frames.

Sixteen

B ut why would I want to move? Summers at Southerly were gorgeous, and at that time of year, I loved being there. Everybody wanted to come for the weekend to be near the water, so I was usually surrounded by friends. And if there were no humans, I had my ever-expanding circle of pets to keep me company.

I found Lily, my first pug, when I foolishly walked into a New York City pet store to see the puppies. I spotted a mischievous puppy creating havoc wherever she went. She just wanted to play and be loved. And that face! She had beautiful chocolate eyes that were so expressive. I simply had to have her. I left the store with Lily. We didn't know about puppy mills then—that unscrupulous breeders were abusively churning out dogs for profit with no concern for the animal's health. That's how Lily came into the world, and she suffered from multiple medical problems as a result, but she was the sweetest dog, loved by all.

I had the same immediate reaction when I found two miniature horses desperately in need of a home. I've always loved miniature horses, so when a friend who owned an enormous sporting estate on Long Island offered to give me two from her stable, I thought I might take them. Coincidentally, I stopped at a filling station and noticed a crude little cement stable with a tin roof at the back of the property.

When I looked inside, I saw two adorable miniature horses, both gray. Someone had tossed in a little hay and a bucket of water. These darlings were in tough shape, and I knew there and then that I couldn't leave them to this sad existence. They needed to be rescued . . . *immediately.* I bought them and took them to an equine vet, who cleaned them and trimmed their hooves. Amazingly, they turned out to be rare Appaloosas—a male and a female.

I named them Maggie and Beauregard and built a miniature paddock and chinoiserie stable for their home. I even had a mini-cart to take them out for mini-trots. I drove them all over Centre Island and made friends with other people in the area who had miniature horses. Maggie and Beauregard thrived and became romantically inclined.

Maggie's first pregnancy didn't go well, so I was a little nervous about her second. When the equine vet told me the birth was imminent, maybe two weeks away, I sent Maggie to a famous horse hospital so she could get proper medical attention. She had nursing care around the clock for what turned out to be three months. That birth wasn't so imminent, after all. And when the foal arrived, it needed knee surgery. The bill was astronomical, but mother and baby were thankfully fine.

With the animals, the beautiful grounds, and the tranquil water, Southerly was positively bucolic during the warm months. But in the winter . . . brrrr! It was hard to say what was more punishing— the snow, the black ice, or the bone-chilling wind whipping off Long Island Sound. I remember taking Lily out to pee. First, I'd bundle up in a fur coat, hat, mittens, and boots. Then, I'd drag her outside to look for a spot. Lily was very particular and could never find the place that was just right. Usually, we paced for about twenty minutes before she was motivated to get the job done. By that time, I was either shivering or numb as a corpse.

And my (literally) fair-weather friends had no desire to venture into the wild when the temperatures plummeted. Southerly in January was the last place they wanted to be. Whitney lived in Los Angeles, where he was pursuing a career in film, so I didn't get to see him as often as I wanted.

The truth is that I was lonely. When Arthur was with me, I never minded the harsh winter weather or the occasional money-pit catastrophe on the property. Everything was an adventure we'd get through together. Now, being alone at Southerly was a constant reminder of his absence. I just wasn't sure what to do about it.

I had an epiphany one day when I was with Rupert Murdoch, who was still my neighbor on Centre Island. "We pay the highest taxes of anybody in the United States," he complained. "I'm going to sell my house."

If he's saying that about New York taxes, and he's Rupert Murdoch, what am I doing with two places in New York? It was a good question.

In addition to paying high taxes, I spent a fortune maintaining Southerly, and the Long Island winters were getting colder every year. I started dreaming about having a place down South. But where? I ruled out Palm Beach because it was like New York with sunshine and palm trees—populated by the same people, all transplants from New York—which can be boring.

And while it was in the South, it wasn't really Southern. The glitz quotient was high, evidenced by the title of the *Shiny Sheet*, the local newspaper that reported on Palm Beach society. And the food was exactly what I would find on the Upper East Side of New York, but I longed for hush puppies and fried tomatoes. I wanted to experience the world of my past, not re-create my present. I'd have to do some serious research to find the right house in an authentically Southern place.

In 2005, Michael Kelcourse and I set off on road trips to visit promising properties in Virginia, Georgia, and the eastern shore of Maryland, and sometimes Mario joined us on these expeditions. I approached each house optimistically, but nothing was quite right, and I wasn't wild about the locations—until I started looking in Charleston. I had spent a lot of time there with Ed when we did the Loop, and I knew the city well. Because Charleston was the fourth largest city in Colonial America and the wealthiest, it boasted a panorama of Southern history. The Battery was particularly appealing with its cobblestone streets and water views. The city had a sense of place, a personality all its own, and a tropical climate that promised sunny days and warm breezes—unless there was a storm or a hurricane. Charleston had plenty of those, too, but I saw the city through my rose-colored glasses and was blind to anything but its genteel beauty.

I was driving through Charleston with my Realtor when the perfect house appeared. Although in the city, the house stood alone on a large plot of land surrounded by a brick wall and was a Roman revival fronted by massive columns. My Realtor explained that it was the Isaac Jenkins Mikell house, built by a wealthy planter in 1853 as a gift for his third wife. Unfortunately, it was not for sale. I spent another year looking at properties, but nothing else called to me.

When I started to despair that I would never find my new home, the Isaac Jenkins Mikell house suddenly appeared on the market, and Mario and I raced to Charleston to see it. The "urban plantation," as it was called, was wonderful and horrible, and those stone walls had quite a story to tell. After the Mikells lived there in grand style, the house became the Charleston Free Library for the next thirty years. Then, it was divided into two residences, and over time had fallen into disrepair. On the plus side, there was a cottage a few feet away from the main house that would be a perfect home for Michael.

Mario looked past the dingy interior and overgrown gardens and announced that the house had beautiful bones. I was quick to jump on the bandwagon and say something totally insane. "It just needs a little painting," was my irrational assessment. *A little painting?* How about a gut renovation? I wanted the house *now* and told myself I'd be practical later. I sold Southerly, stored most of my possessions, and moved to Charleston.

I had to say goodbye to Maggie and Beau, who couldn't come with me to Charleston because the city classified them as livestock, meaning they were prohibited from living at a residence. I found them a good home on a farm, where the owner dotes on them. I think she even curls their eyelashes. Maggie is blind, but her dutiful daughter leads her everywhere, and Beau is doing well. I miss them, but they're leading a good life.

We arrived in Charleston with great expectations until reality set in. All old houses have secrets, but this one was a Russian doll of surprises. Nothing worked. Everything needed to be replaced. It was a long labor of love for me; my talented architect, Lewis Graeber; and, of course, Mario, and it seemed as if a million choices were to be made as we reconfigured the layout and restored the rooms.

The "before" pictures were terrifying. The bathroom in the primary suite had old, rusty fixtures and dank walls that looked like the backdrop for a drug deal about to go wrong. Outside, the gardens were overgrown, and the pool needed extensive work. If anyone thinks I'm a delicate flower, they should think again. For the year-and-a-half-long restoration, I lived like a squatter on the construction site, moving my bed, lamp, and bridge table to whatever room in the house wasn't under attack. Most days, I was in the company of twenty-five to thirty workers, who filled 125 dumpsters with rubble.

When the construction was finished, Mario assembled a team of experts to transform the house. He came to Charleston at least ten times and was *my* emotional support animal. Designing a 9,500-square-foot home with twenty rooms requires a superhuman imagination. The house was too dark and, in Mario's words, had "a frumpy beige interior." But not for long. "Let there be light" was his mantra.

Three people on scaffolds spent six months turning the walls into faux marble. Mario decided to glaze the double drawing room walls with a luminous shade of apple green, which he mixed on-site and had the floors in the entrance hall painted white and finished with a trompe l'oeil pattern. Then came the wallpapers and coverings, including my Zuber panels depicting the Revolutionary War, which were hung in the dining room. Prudence Carter, the trompe l'oeil artist who painted the image of our cat, Sally, on the panel, added my pug, Lily, to the scene. Both of these beloved pets are gone now, but it's very comforting to see their tiny images preserved on the wallpaper. I was honored when Zuber asked me to write about my memories in the foreword to the book *Zuber: Two Centuries of Panoramic Wallpaper*.

Each design choice brought the house closer to what it was meant to be—an airy, light-infused Mediterranean villa complete with lemon trees on the piazza. While the house was beautiful in a formal sense, it was also deeply personal. I hung masterpieces from Arthur's collection alongside my art, including my dog and sporting paintings, and displayed my collection of china pugs on a side table.

I think my collections of pugs, poodles, and whatnots are beautiful, although Whitney has some issues and complains that they're always in the way.

"Get rid of some of the knickknacks," he thunders whenever he knocks one over.

"They're not knickknacks; they're eighteenth century," I argue in their defense.

"Well, they're eighteenth-century knickknacks," he counters.

They're not going anywhere.

I featured my framed silhouettes, which are profiles traced on to and cut from black paper, on the curved wall adjacent to the grand staircase. My parents owned a few when I was growing up, but I paid closer attention to the genre when I was an art adviser and started collecting them when I was in Europe. Arthur and I always looked for silhouettes when we made our rounds of antiques stores in London and Paris. Most of mine are British—the American ones are more primitive. My most valuable one, and my favorite, depicts George Washington. To date, it's his only silhouette that was done from life. I also have one of Robert E. Lee, which was given to me by my second husband, who was his direct descendant.

Wherever I look, I see my mother's French furniture, my father's Chinoiserie, Arthur's paintings—all reminders of my family history, and that's what a home should be. If these rooms could talk!

Comfort is important, too, so my bedroom and bathroom are my favorite rooms in the house. If, like Rapunzel, I found myself imprisoned in my primary suite, I would be perfectly happy. My bathroom has a Jacuzzi tub, a big-screen television, and a fireplace. What more could I want?

Finally, a home should also be conducive to fun. I have three fully stocked bars in various places on the first floor, so a guest is never more than a few steps away from a cocktail.

Mario loved what we accomplished. When we finished, he turned to me and said, "This is my best house."

I agree that it's the greatest thing he's ever done.

Seventeen

I think Charleston is the most beautiful American city that we have. With the architecture, the gardens, the ambiance, the food, and being that close to the water, it has everything. I totally understand why *Travel + Leisure*'s readers ranked it the number one city in the world. When I moved down here, my New York friends thought it was all Honey Boo Boo and Gator Boys because they had never been to the South. It amazed me that they had been to Burma and the Outer Hebrides but had never crossed the Mason-Dixon Line. They couldn't get over how beautiful and sophisticated it was when they visited.

And the people! The descendants of those founders who were fun-loving cavaliers in the eighteenth century are here today, and they still know how to have a good time. They're also exceedingly warm and hospitable. Michael, who could be quite reserved and was used to the ways of brittle New Yorkers, didn't know what to make of the strangers on the street who greeted him with a cheery "Good morning!" He thought their behavior was bizarre until he got used to it and started responding in kind.

Traveling back and forth to New York when I wanted to be in my new home became somewhat onerous, and I started to spend more and more time in Charleston. At a certain point, I realized that Whitney used the New York apartment more than I did and eventually decided to sell it.

Whitney lives in fear that I will tell too many tales about him in this memoir, so I have shown remarkable restraint lest I embarrass him. But there comes a moment when a proud mother feels compelled to recount her remarkable son's many accomplishments; this is where we are.

Whitney moved to Los Angeles after living in London and Paris because he was interested in the film business. It's one of the hardest fields to crack, but I've discovered that when Whitney sets his mind to something, it happens, and in very little time, he started working as a writer, director, and producer. His first film, *Bubba and Ike*, was a raucous comedy about rednecks. Then he made *Torture TV*, starring Danny Huston. These subjects were a little out of my realm, but I found his new project, a documentary about the legendary fashion designer Halston, fascinating. I used to wear Halston and met him once in New York, but there was so much more I wanted to know about him. *Ultrasuede*, named after Halston's favorite fabric, promised to tell the real story.

Whitney arranged to interview many people close to Halston, including Liza Minnelli, Anjelica Huston, Bob Colacello, and model Pat Cleveland, and he also spoke to fashion insiders like André. Their recollections and insights, along with quintessential images of Halston and his glittering world, painted a vivid portrait of the man and his fabulous, turbulent life.

Ultrasuede also marks my screen debut. Being a good son, Whitney asked me to do a cameo in the film, and so there I am in a scene, happily toasting his success. The film premiered in Los Angeles,

London, and New York and made quite a splash at festivals. Whitney scored a coup by selling it to Showtime, where it ran for three years. Then, he concentrated on developing future projects.

After I sold the New York apartment, Whitney began spending more time with me in Charleston, his first experience living in the South. He appreciated the city's beauty and history but was more intrigued by the people who lived there. He found them to be wildly eccentric characters with a charm all their own—a charm that was distinctly Southern. Whitney has a knack for finding the social center of a place, and he became acquainted with a few colorful men in town—Thomas Ravenel and Shep Rose—who were perfect Southern specimens. They were entertaining raconteurs and had a way with the ladies. Better still, they frequently misbehaved.

Thomas, the son of the South Carolina congressman who gave his name to Charleston's Ravenel Bridge, had founded a commercial real estate company before running for state treasurer in 2006. He won the election but was ousted from office after a scandal I won't discuss here. He owned Brookland, a former indigo and cotton plantation on Edisto Island outside of Charleston.

Thomas introduced Whitney to Shep, a South Carolina native from a family with strong historical ties to the state and its traditions. Shep, who describes himself as "overeducated and undermotivated," was drifting, trying to find the next right thing after his post-MBA job at a company in Dubai was derailed by the 2008 recession. Maybe real estate, maybe hospitality, maybe a hot dog stand, but in the meantime, Shep was very successful at having a good time, and his sunny, surfer personality inspired others to do the same.

Whitney also met Craig Conover, who had graduated from the College of Charleston and attended the Charleston School of Law. Like Shep, he was contemplating his future. He was young enough to know how to have fun but old enough to know he should be thinking about his next moves.

These men were single, good-looking, privileged, and steeped in the ways of the South. Initially, Whitney imagined making a documentary film about Thomas, with the new Charleston social scene as background, but later decided the subject would work better with a larger canvas and a continuing story. He reconfigured the concept as a reality television show chronicling the adventures, misadventures, and mating rituals of freewheeling Charleston socialites—a combination of *Animal House* and *Downton Abbey*. As he told the *New York Times*, he wanted to create a show that would "deconstruct the myths of the old South but do it in a very funny assertive way." He called it *Southern Charm*.

The genius of his idea was that he would focus on male behavior, the inner workings of the "bro" culture, and the dramas that play out among men as they navigate friendships and romantic relationships. We *expect* the Real Housewives to open up and reveal all, but this would be an opportunity to see men on the hot seat and decode *their* mating habits. If it sounds anthropological, in a way, it is.

Of course, there would be women in the mix, preferably contemporary Southern belles. The first season introduced Cameran Eubanks, who grew up in South Carolina and previously starred on the show *The Real World*; Jenna King, an aspiring fashion designer; and Kathryn Dennis, a descendant of vice president John C. Calhoun and the granddaughter of Rembert C. Dennis, an influential South Carolina political figure.

Bravo loved the concept and greenlit the show, promoting Charleston as "a playground for men who never want to grow up." That wasn't the Charleston I knew, but I was happy for Whitney.

Before *Southern Charm*, I had never watched reality TV, so I wasn't knowledgeable about the genre or how it worked. When they started shooting, I learned more than I wanted to know. One day, the crew came to my house to film a few scenes with Whitney, and suddenly, hordes of people toting heavy equipment walked over my painted floors and taped cords to my faux marble walls. I was terrified for my furniture, paintings, and porcelain. Michael, being a responsible butler, was apoplectic. Had Mario been there, he would have killed them.

Whitney saw how anxious I was and tried to reassure me. He said, "Look, Mother, why don't you just relax and film for five minutes? That's all you'll have to do. I'll work on finding another location so you don't have all this happening in the house."

That's what he said: *Five minutes, and you're done.*

Well, we know how *that* went. We're filming our tenth season as I write.

Eighteen

M y first appearance on *Southern Charm* was impromptu . . . and reluctant. I would have agreed to anything to get the crew out of the house as quickly as possible. With my microphone in place, I walked into my son's room while he played the guitar because the amplifier was so loud that the second floor vibrated. Whitney is a wonderful musician, a classically trained guitarist. But whenever he starts to shred metal, he must be stopped before heads explode, specifically, *my* head. This happens frequently.

We bantered about the pile of cheap women's clothing I spied on the bedroom floor, evidence of a sleepover date who had absolutely no taste. Annoyed, Whitney suggested it might be time for him to move to a "stabbin' cabin." A "stabbin' cabin"? Clearly, they spoke a different language in this brave new Bravo world, and I needed an urban dictionary to learn the meaning of *bitch slap*, *throwing shade*, and *showmance*. What Whitney was saying was that he would look for an apartment.

When we finished filming our scene, I had to admit I enjoyed our repartee. I'd said whatever popped into my head, and it was fun!

Gradually, I became a regular on *Southern Charm* with a defined role. Just as Whitney imagined when he conceived the show, the guys and the girls channeled *Animal House* with their sexcapades, feuds, and over-the-top behavior, and I paid homage to *Downton Abbey* by playing the Dowager Countess of Charleston. And all I had to do was be myself.

"Let the games begin" was my attitude when I began working with the other Charmers. Contrary to what my son might think, I was young once, a hundred years ago. But my castmates weren't just younger than me; they were a completely different species. I was never like them when I was their age. I got married when I was twenty. I was serious about graduate school. I worked hard and was dedicated to being ambitious and making something of myself, so their behavior was incomprehensible.

Many of the people on the show seemed happy to, shall we say, coast and live in the moment. The guys let other people do all the work, and if they had a problem, they dipped into their trust funds to solve it. Some of the girls had no apparent careers, and their "ambitions" were not the kind I endorse—one showed up in a skirt so short that I observed her "ambition" was showing. I can't relate to any of that, so I make snarky comments about how being a reprobate doesn't get you very far. I tease and chide them when they need it—which seems to be all the time.

Then I give them advice, whether or not they ask for it, and which they totally ignore. This has been our dynamic since the first season. I'm Mother Knows Best to the Little Rascals. But I do get a kick out of them and find them fun. And I think being around younger people keeps you young.

What I enjoy most about the show is that I get to speak my mind. My reactions are genuine and uncensored. There are so many times when I could take the high road and keep my opinions to myself. But I don't, because the high road sometimes isn't as interesting. In the words of my friends who have a popular podcast about all things Bravo, it's much more fun to say anything and "watch what crappens."

What "crappened" during the first season was reality TV gold. To recap, Kathryn Dennis, the youngest person on the show, dated Thomas, who was twenty-nine years her senior, and got pregnant. However, there was a moment when she wasn't sure if Thomas or Shep fathered the baby. Ultimately, Thomas won that particular paternity lottery.

Being a stranger to the baby-mama culture, if I can call it that, I had thoughts and plenty of them, and recalled the prevailing sentiment when I was growing up.

"In my day," I said, "if you got knocked up, you went to a home for unwed mothers, and your parents changed their name and moved to Missoula."

Clearly, this was not the case today. Judgment aside, Kathryn and Thomas had a beautiful daughter. Although I did tell Thomas that "instead of impregnating twenty-one-year-olds, you might refocus, is all I'm suggesting." He didn't listen to my advice because, in season 3, Kathryn got pregnant a second time. Their storyline was the gift that just kept giving.

Another never-ending story was the merry-go-round of hookups on the show. I would need a Venn diagram to chart *Southern Charm*'s various flirtations, one-night stands, love affairs, and breakups. Let's just say that all roads lead to Kathryn, Austen Kroll, and Shep. It doesn't pay for me to get too specific. If you watch the show, you know—and if not, you probably don't care. But I find the constant recycling a mystery, especially when the motivation for hooking up with a friend's current or ex-partner is revenge.

We didn't have revenge sex in my day—we had revenge *marriage*, meaning if you want to get back at a caddish boyfriend, find someone better and marry them. Which makes much more of an impact.

There's a question I ask myself at some point during every season, and, as I said, we've now had ten. There are a zillion attractive young people in Charleston. Why this group insists on fishing in the same pond and sleeping with each other is beyond me. It's very incestuous, right out of *Peyton Place*. Maybe they should get out more.

I also wonder why the show is classified as "reality TV" when so many of the developments are *surreal*. Are the Charmers inherently over-the-top, or do the cameras fan the flame? Whatever the cause, their behavior gives me ample opportunities to comment, and rarely with approval.

To be fair, I'm just as critical of Whitney as I am of everyone else. My son never gets a free pass. Fortunately, he has a sense of humor, which I'd like to think he gets from me. How else could he tolerate my very public takedowns of his personal life? I have made no secret of my desire for him to get married and have children. His presence in Charleston has given me a front-row seat to the smorgasbord of women in his life. Some were lovely, but others fell squarely into the "bless her heart" category.

"Bless her/his heart" is an expression Southerners use as a stealth insult. The words sound sweet, but they're candy-coated condemnation, usually directed at someone who has done something stupid or wrong-minded. Another expression that's even more deadly is "I'll pray for you." I reserve that for the Internet trolls who send barbed comments my way. One of Whitney's dates, the clueless model who walked into the house, admired my Post-Impressionist paintings and announced that her favorite artist was "Moët," like the champagne, and earned a rousing "bless her heart." So did the Russian oligarch's daughter, who came for an extended stay with her untrained puppy and expected me to watch it.

Mothers dream of the perfect mate for their son, someone who is beautiful inside and out and educated (preferably with a degree in art history, but that's just me being selfish). I'm so desperate for a grandchild that I've cut my wish list to the bone: I'll settle for anyone who walks upright.

But going back to the start of it all, I insulted his "stabbin' cabin"—a dreary brown loft filled with ugly, oversize furniture—by calling it a dump, and it truly was. I told him his ambition to open a restaurant was pedestrian and banal because I knew he could do more. Whenever I'm judgmental, Whitney responds to my remarks with a lot of eye-rolling. He likes to say that putting me on the show was the worst mistake he ever made and that I'm giving him ulcers, but I don't think he means it.

Quips aside, I admire everything about my son and am proud of his accomplishments. He's a gentleman—old-school in the best ways—and he's also brilliant, creative, and hardworking. I want to emphasize this because not all the cast members on *Southern Charm* share his work ethic. They're much more interested in debauchery.

I wanted the show, his brainchild, to succeed, and naturally, I wondered how it would be received. *Southern Charm* had the benefit of national publicity and promotion before it launched. Bravo ran ads continuously because the network believed the show would draw a big audience. There were articles everywhere, a billboard in Times Square, and posters on buses in major cities, all generating big buzz. *Southern Charm* fulfilled its promise and became a hit overnight, drawing more viewers every time it aired.

Curiously, here in Charleston, where it all happened, crickets.

Charlestonians feigned disdain and predicted *Southern Charm* would be a disaster for the city because it showed Southerners in a bad light and didn't accurately portray the place or the people who lived there. "A pop culture smear on the Holy City," lambasted one local critic. Weirdly, people who claimed they had never watched the show were full of opinions about the characters and the plotline. Of course, *everyone* watched it—or hate-watched—but snobbishly pretended that they didn't.

That changed pretty quickly. With each season, the show has grown in popularity. Despite the initial cold shoulder from Charlestonians, now they praise us for bringing in hundreds of millions of tourist dollars. Charleston, a city that has always been popular, is a destination for fans who want to experience the *Southern Charm* lifestyle firsthand. There are dedicated *Southern Charm* walking tours to see the various sites shown in the series, and the carriage tours have added my house to their itineraries.

Fans flock to the house, and the bold ones climb the wall to get a closer look. They wave to me while I'm sitting on the piazza, and if I see them, I wave back. Whenever I go out, I have my hair and makeup done because twenty to thirty people could be standing outside, jostling to take pictures of the house, which became a celebrity after it was voted "Best House on Reality TV." At the airport, I have to allow extra time for selfie requests. Everybody is very kind, respectful, and appreciative. I haven't been called a meddling old bag . . . yet.

I've also been recognized in England and other places because *Southern Charm* is seen in more than twenty countries. My favorite encounter with an international fan occurred in a ladies' room in Jaipur, India. I was talking to a friend, and a woman in one of the stalls recognized my voice and raced out to meet me. And this was in *India.*

On the night of the show's second season premiere in 2015, Andy Cohen reported on *Watch What Happens Live* that Lady Gaga tweeted, "Patricia on #SouthernCharm, like lookin' in the damn mirror. Cheers queen." He was so excited, and I was very flattered. Although, quite frankly, I didn't know who Lady Gaga was. I do now!

Ask Me Anything:

Manners Edition

Table manners are so important. How can we teach children—and some adults—to behave properly at the table?

If you set a good example when children are young, they'll emulate you. I'd stress the basics—sit up straight, put a napkin in your lap, keep your elbows off the table, use the correct utensils, and never chew with your mouth open. And the most important rule is not to use electronic devices, toys, and other distractions during meals. No cell phones at the table!

Help! I'm in my twenties, and like most people my age, I usually eat take-out. I'm invited to a formal dinner party, and I'm afraid I won't know how to use all that dinnerware!

Don't worry. A formal place setting is very logical because it is organized according to the order in which the implements will be used. On the left, the smaller salad fork comes first, then the dinner fork. On the right, glasses are lined up according to their function, beginning with the water glass and proceeding to the wineglasses. If you're confused about which bread plate and glasses are yours, try this simple trick. Rest your hands on the table and make an "OK" sign with both index fingers and thumbs. The left hand will look like the letter *b* for *bread*, while the right hand will look like the letter *d* for *drink*. Now you know exactly what to do.

What's the best way to start a conversation with someone you don't know?
I can tell you what I *don't* do. When I meet someone for the first time, I never ask what they do for a living because the question may make them uncomfortable. What if they don't work, or they're between situations? Instead, I say, "Tell me about yourself," which gives the person the opportunity to shape their own story. In my experience, people love talking about themselves, so the conversation will be off to a good start.

Is there a graceful way to get someone to tell you their name when you know you've met them before but can't remember who they are?
We all wish we had the handy assistants in *The Devil Wears Prada* who whisper in Miranda Priestly's ear when she doesn't recognize someone. The rest of us have to figure it out on our own. I greet the person warmly and say, "Please remind me of your name." When they respond with their first name (which they usually do), I tell them, "No, not your first name, I know that. Your *last* name." It works every time.

We've all been trapped in a conversation that never ends at a cocktail party. What's your graceful exit line when you're ready to move on?
I always say the same thing. "You'll have to excuse me. I'm running to the ladies' room." Nobody can say anything about *that*, and you're off the hook.

I struggle to find the right words when I write a thank-you note. What's the best way to begin, and how long should it be?

The first step is to always have appropriate stationery and stamps on hand. You can order lovely stamps from usps.com. I like to use engraved cards (4½ x 6½) with matching envelopes for thank-you notes. You should start by expressing your thanks and describing the gift with a few choice words, saying what you like about it. Do it right away, while you still feel grateful, and keep it short—no one expects a magnum opus. They'll be touched that you took the time to write and send a personal note.

What's the proper (and most becoming) way for a woman to sit—legs crossed or uncrossed?

There are two options. My mother told me to press my knees together and cross my ankles. Or you can do what's called the "duchess slant." The ladies in the royal family press their knees and ankles together, then slant their legs.

Nineteen

‏⁓•⁓

I'm often asked if the show is scripted. The answer should be obvious because no writer on the planet could make this stuff up. The pyrotechnics on *Southern Charm* are fueled by spontaneous combustion. Rub two Charmers together, and there are bound to be sparks—if not fireworks. As for the storylines, no one could script Kathryn's pregnancies, Craig's pivot from lawyer to pillow king, or a hurricane disrupting a party I had spent weeks planning. When the camera rolls, stuff happens, and happens, and happens. The drama is real, and the "characters" are often a part of my real life.

Even when we're not filming, Shep, Craig, and Austen are fixtures at the house. They come over to have a beer and hang out with Whitney. I'm like the den mother at a halfway house. My mother always said you are the company you keep, so it looks like I'm a B-list f###boy! But I find the boys—if I can still call them that—amusing, so I don't mind them being underfoot. Every year, I think, *You all will get over your Peter Pan syndrome.* But somehow, like a landfill, their juvenile behavior never goes away.

I've always enjoyed Cameran and her husband, Jason, who's a lovely man and a skilled physician. Cameran was different from the other women on the show. First of all, she's happily married, so she was not a part of the turbulent singles scene that consumed the other cast members every waking minute. She's down-to-earth, genuinely supportive of her friends, and stays above the petty dramas. I've always found her life very relatable because we see her grappling with insecurities about her career, motherhood, and other real-life issues. I don't see her as often as I'd like because she's busy with her family, but we're still friends.

My relationship with Madison LeCroy actually predated the show. Madison joined *Southern Charm* in season 6 because she was dating Austen, who became a Charmer in season 4, but I've been friends with her for eighteen years. When I first met her, she was the tireless shampoo assistant at the salon where I had my hair done. Madison spent all her free time learning, even when she was nine months pregnant with her first child and later when she was going through a divorce.

I always admired her for her work ethic, talent, and great outlook and watched her come up through the ranks, from doing simple blowouts to coloring and cuts. Then, she became the best hairstylist in Charleston. She jokes about how I rarely recommend her to others because I wanted her to be available when *I* needed her. She's not wrong about that.

Madison doesn't do hair anymore because she has so many endorsements and business interests. Thankfully, we still get to spend time together. Not only is she beautiful, but she's also very funny. Lately, we've been discussing the idea of doing a podcast together because we never run out of things to talk about.

We were all surprised when the breakout star of *Southern Charm* turned out to be Michael, known as Michael the Butler, who accomplishes so much by saying so little. He was the classic straight man, impassive in the face of high jinks and debauchery. Calm and capable in his signature red apron, Michael became the resident expert on cocktails and everything domestic, and so many fans wrote to him for his housekeeping advice that we had to incorporate an "Ask Michael" button on my website. They also asked questions about me, wanting to know if I was nice or a cranky old bitch. I think they were hoping to hear the latter.

Michael was a star in real life, too, although he never sought recognition for his private acts of kindness. One story stands out: Michael took my pug Chauncey to the veterinarian for an appointment and encountered a young woman sobbing in the waiting room. Her dog was dying, but she couldn't afford the cost of a treatment that might extend his life. Michael, the ultimate pet lover, stepped in to help. He quietly went to the front desk and arranged to pay for the treatment (which turned out to cost thousands of dollars), anonymously—he was incredibly generous that way.

I like to think that Michael and I made the martini great again. When I say, "It's time for my medicine," everyone knows exactly what I mean. A gin martini is a form of medicine—gin contains botanicals, including juniper, lemon peel, coriander seed, almond, Seville orange peel, orris root, licorice root, angelica root, and angelica seed. No wonder they're so restorative, although that may have something to do with gin being about 80 proof.

I wish everyone could experience Michael's extraordinary martini, but most will never have the pleasure, so I'm sharing his signature recipe here. Don't even think about not using the ice bag and mallet, the secret to Michael's success.

Michael's Martini

- Place gin and vermouth (ratio of 1 to 2, or 2 to 3) in a shaker. Fill a shaker with ice. Let sit.

- Using the Lewis ice mallet and bag, crush a new batch of ice into splinters and place in a glass almost to the top—add an olive or a twist of lemon. Give the shaker two or three good shakes (if filming, do it with a flourish) and pour into the glass.

- Sip appreciatively.

People sometimes ask me, "Why are you hanging out with these youngsters?" (A thought that's crossed *my* mind more than once.) "Don't you have any friends of your own?" Well, I have numerous friends—women, men, gay, straight, single, and married—and I'm lucky to have such a diverse group. They're fabulous, and they love *Southern Charm.* They all think it's hilarious and a big hoot. As the show evolved, I made it a point to invite my friends to film with us. Georgette Mosbacher was a natural—she was probably camera-ready the day she was born. When she came to Charleston, I hosted a cast dinner to celebrate the launch of our caftan company, an idea we conceived on a trip to India.

People are fascinated by my caftans—I often say that I have more than Lawrence of Arabia (André loved them, too. He liked to say, "I have more than ten and less than fifty . . . I'm not Marie-Antoinette.")—so here's a little backstory. I've worn caftans for years and was inspired by the iconic women who modeled them in the 1960s. Elizabeth Taylor adorned them with exquisite jewels. Marella Agnelli, the essence of Italian elegance, wore them at her villa. Talitha

Getty, the bohemian It Girl, made them a must-have garment for fashionable free spirits everywhere.

Caftans became even more important to me after I moved to Charleston. Instead of wearing little black dresses and high heels—a uniform in New York—the women here, especially the young ones, wear cutoff T-shirts, raggy shorts, and flip-flops and blame it on the heat. I decided there had to be another way to embrace casual dress without looking like a hot mess, and a caftan was the answer. They're chic, comfortable, conceal a multitude of sins, and are my go-to choice when I entertain. The woman in the caftan is always the life of the party, which probably explains why I have so many—but never enough.

When Georgette and I went on our Thelma-and-Louise trip to India, we met with Sherina Dalamal, a talented and successful wedding dress designer. We had a motive. We told her we had two loves, caftans and dogs. At the time, I had my Pomeranians Siegfried and Roy, Chauncey the pug, Monty the Lagotto, and Whitney's dog, Smoochie. Georgette was devoted to her dog, Guinevere, a Cavalier King Charles spaniel. We explained to Sherina that we thought it would be fun to have a caftan with the image of a favorite pet on it (which meant that I would need at least *five* canine-themed caftans).

Sherina made a customized caftan for Georgette with a silk-screened image of Guinevere. I got one printed with Chauncey's sweet face. The response from fellow pet lovers was so enthusiastic that we started a company, Patricia's Couture, to meet the demand, hence our celebratory dinner party on the show. I asked my castmates to dress appropriately for the Indian-themed dinner, preferably in saris. Georgette and I went to the dogs and wore our new caftans. I decorated the dining room table with elephants and arranged for an Indian fortune teller to come after dinner.

Georgette took control immediately. She's like a four-star general, and she intimidates everybody. I find it amusing that people are afraid of her. In her draconian way, she announced that there would be no four-letter words or conversations about money, politics, or sex at the table. There was a collective gasp. With *this* group, there might be nothing left to say.

During dinner, Georgette offered some relationship advice. She's a master at decoding the complicated "men are from Mars, women are from Venus" dynamics between men and women. Everyone was surprised when she emphasized the importance of forgiveness and setting aside petty grievances. Her good advice resonated because *Southern Charm* is all about fighting and forgetting. I have a hard time remembering who's feuding with whom, and sometimes it's *me*. Everyone was on their best behavior until they weren't, and tempers flared. Typically, the f-words started to fly. Never one to suffer fools lightly, Georgette raised her eyebrows, expressed her disapproval, and made a dramatic exit.

Georgette has high standards, and she's a woman of her word. I love that about her.

Mario appeared on the show several times, and he was an impish presence—maybe even a ham. In one early episode, he came to the house to put the finishing touches on my bedroom. Rocky, my cat, had just passed away, and Mario suggested I put his ashes in a Delft jar and place it on a shelf over my bed. I loved Rocky, and rarely disagreed with Mario, but this time, *no, thank you.*

On another occasion, he eyed Whitney's fashionably slim-cut pants and announced, "Those trousers look like a cheap hotel."

When Whitney seemed puzzled by his assessment, Mario delivered his wicked punch line. "There's no ballroom."

Mario had friends and fans everywhere, but he was most

excited when someone recognized him from his appearances on the show.

Some of my friends may have been more advanced in years than the "youngsters" on *Southern Charm*, but they had character and personality. What's the proverb? "Old is gold."

I enjoy the show most when I host a dinner or a cocktail party, which is what I do best. When my castmates entertain on the show, I'm usually served warm chardonnay, to which I say, "One cannot drink cheap wine in the heat," and I'm likely to see bags of chips that look like they've been opened by squirrels. And soda cans stuffed with cigarette butts. That never happens at my house, where we take parties very seriously.

I love a good theme—a flamingo party, where everything, including the champagne, is pink, or a Kentucky Derby party with authentic mint juleps. Then there's the gentlemen's dinner I host regularly for Whitney and his friends. I fall into the same trap every time. I plan an impressive meal, set a beautiful table, and try to elevate the conversation, imagining *this* will be the night when boys become men . . . but they don't. What's more likely to happen is that one bro insults another, leading to fisticuffs; Craig breaks a valuable antique chair; and Whitney serves a rare bottle of bourbon that turns out to be 200-proof rocket fuel that sends everyone into outer space. So much for fantasizing about a gathering of young Cary Grants.

The advantage of appearing on a hit television show is that, sometimes, I can use *Southern Charm* to promote awareness about the charities I support. In season 2, I organized an event to raise money for the Wounded Warrior Project, a cause that is close to my heart. I come from a long line of military men I could trace back all the way to the Revolutionary War. I greatly admire those who have served, and I think we should do more for our returning veterans. A fundraiser, which would be filmed for the show, could bring together the cast and members of the community to show our appreciation for our soldiers.

Charleston is home to the Patriots Point Naval and Maritime Museum, and the jewel in its crown is the USS *Yorktown*. Known as the "Fighting Lady," the historic aircraft carrier played a pivotal role in the Pacific theater during World War II. It was decommissioned in 1970 and sent to Charleston to serve as a memorial to its heroic past. Whenever I see the *Yorktown* in the harbor, I think of my father, who spent most of his adult life on navy ships in that very part of the world.

I planned an event that included cocktails on the flight deck, a performance by country pop singer Kelsea Ballerini, and an auction. We have really cute guys on the show, so why not let people bid on a date with Craig or Shep? Kelsea surprised everyone by bidding $5,000 for Craig. Shep, who was auction item number two, failed to elicit such a dramatic response and was crestfallen until Cameran came to his rescue with a winning bid. The competition fanned the flames of their fraternal rivalry, but it was all in fun and for a good cause—and we raised a lot of money.

Is there a downside to appearing on a reality TV show? What keeps me up at night has nothing to do with the endless drama; the now-you-see-them, now-you-don't relationships; the scandals; and the potential for reputational damage. I don't really worry about my reputation. When you're my age, you know who you are, and nothing can change that. Although I don't want anyone putting up ugly paparazzi pictures of me.

What I can't bear is the ongoing agony of having a camera crew in my house. All that heavy equipment is an accident waiting to happen, and I've already lived through a few bull-in-the-china-shop incidents. I watched helplessly as a camera crashed through an irreplaceable panel of eighteenth-century glass. I had to say goodbye to an antique Irish decanter that had belonged to my father after a camera operator knocked it off a shelf. The possibility of disaster is always with us, even though the production crew tries to be *really* careful. Broken hearts are one thing. They can mend. But broken antiques? Unacceptable.

Twenty

Thanks to my tenure at *Southern Charm*, my world expanded in so many interesting and unexpected ways. If I imagined I'd spend my golden years relaxing and reminiscing about the past like a better-dressed Miss Havisham, it was not to be.

You'd think that preaching about the death of civility and the end of Western civilization would make me a dinosaur—that annoying "in my day" crank who invokes the glories of a distant past that absolutely no one remembers. Instead, I discovered I had become a modern Miss Manners and a tastemaker for viewers of all ages who enjoyed my critiques of contemporary lifestyles, especially when I called out inappropriate behavior.

Minding your manners in the twenty-first century can be very tricky because it is not something we're taught anymore. Fans, journalists from *Vogue*, *Town & Country*, *The New York Times*, and other publications, as well as bloggers and influencers came to me for advice on how to behave, which prompted me to write *The Art of Southern Charm*, an anecdotal guide to having a beautiful life. The book covered everything from hosting a party to organizing a closet or writing a thank-you note (yes, you need stationery and stamps). And I paid special attention to affairs of the heart—love, marriage, and everything in between because, with three marriages behind me, I have had extensive experience.

Suddenly, I became known as "Miss Patricia," a nod, I hope, to my being *wise*, not wizened. To be clear, I never wanted to lay down the law in a schoolmarmish way. And I am not, and have never been, a snob. Fun is where you find it, and I can find it anywhere, at Versailles or Costco. But I feared that many of the niceties I had grown up practicing were in danger of becoming extinct, and I wanted to introduce them to a new generation. They still worked for me, and I believed they could enhance other lives.

Some principles are obvious. Say please and thank you. Hold open the damn door for the next person. Stand up when a woman enters the room. *Never* use a cell phone at the table.

Some are arcane, but good to know. Yes, you can (and should) eat asparagus with your fingers. Just be sure to remove your evening gloves before you pick up a stalk.

And what about wardrobe and grooming? Some of the women who appeared on *Southern Charm* needed a feature-length tutorial, prompting me to observe, "Women today look like they've been shot out of a cannon." My advice to them was to avoid trends, buy quality clothes, and maintain them beautifully. And yes, there are occasions when you can wear a tiara. In the words of Oscar Wilde, "You can never be overdressed or overeducated."

A fulsome vocabulary is important, too. I'm sure that the words *skank* and *ho* say it all in some circles, but I like peppering my speech with more erudite choices. I take full credit for breathing new life into the word *strumpet*—and, no, a strumpet is not a hybrid pastry like a cronut. It's a Middle English word that describes a loose woman, as in shameless strumpet.

Speaking of *shameless*, I'm mystified by some of the dating and courtship rituals practiced today. I expressed my incredulity in my first book, and I wasn't afraid to make suggestions that might be considered old-fashioned in a time of OkCupid.

I think the best way to meet someone is through mutual friends. It worked for me three times.

Have a real conversation rather than exchange verbal résumés: flirting shouldn't be the third degree.

And unless you're trying to keep your address a secret (in which case, why are you going out with someone you wouldn't want to have that information?), expect your date to escort you home at the end of the evening regardless of whether a sleepover is on the menu.

Be prepared to kiss a lot of frogs. Finding a soulmate is never easy.

And if you do meet the *one*, have the hard conversations before you get in too deep. Knowing your potential mate's Starbucks preference or golf handicap is less important than being informed about his or her spending habits and financial goals. Money is not a four-letter word.

I could list a dozen additional caveats, although I suspected my advice would fall on deaf ears. Interestingly, the same people who thought nothing of texting an eggplant emoji to a prospective date were intrigued by my retro approach to mating. Like being "sober curious," they wanted to experiment with a different approach, and I gave them something to think about.

I have opinions about everything, and I covered a broad spectrum of topics in the book. To round out my advice, I asked my friends who were talented in different ways to share their expertise about life management, cooking, courtship, style, and home decor.

My first call was to Joan DiPietro, my personal assistant, who can organize anything and has kept my life orderly for more than twenty years. I hired her after Arthur died because I needed someone to handle the perplexing administrative details that threatened to overwhelm me—bill paying, spreadsheets, tax preparation, scheduling, invitations, curatorial work. I was drowning in paper until Joan came and brought order to chaos. She set up systems that work, which is no small feat.

Anyone can follow her commonsense advice for managing the business of life. As boring as it is to do, maintain good old-fashioned files. Keep a daybook of appointments to track tax-deductible expenses. And take care of mail as it comes in every day because it doesn't get better with age.

Katie Lee, cookbook author and hostess extraordinaire, told all the single ladies who want to impress their dates with their culinary skills that the surefire way to a man's heart is a big rib eye steak—rare, please. And bake chocolate cookies before they come for dinner because the toasty, brown sugar scent is an aphrodisiac.

Carolyne Roehm, who has never met a table she couldn't set and has ten stunning books on decor to prove it, advised the color-challenged to rely on blue and white to make the table pop.

Carson Kressley, the Emmy-winning television star and author of *Does this Book Make My Butt Look Big?*, reminded us that "only whores and children wear red shoes." Hmmm. I must check my closet.

Georgette, in her very Georgette way, was succinct. To have a real connection with someone, look them in the eye, be open-minded, even adventurous, and never be afraid to compromise.

Of course I turned to Mario for his thoughts on home decor.

"Forget about instant gratification," said the man who enjoyed watching paint dry. "A great room is an investment in time and money."

I shared my advice about entertaining. The *New York Post* interviewed me for tips on hosting an authentic Kentucky Derby party, which, given my lifelong love of horses and affinity for all things Southern, is my signature celebration. Here's how I do it. My handwritten invitations (no calls, no emails) go out in March. Guests are advised to wear "derby attire," which prompts a broad interpretation, but Derby die-hards know to show up in seersucker suits and pastel dresses. Hats are not required, I stressed, because Southern women don't like to flatten their big hair.

I like a classic decor. The derby is also known as the Run for the Roses, so I place vases filled with roses at the food stations. I serve classic Southern finger food so guests can move from room to room (or bar to bar), nibbling along the way—ham biscuits, tea sandwiches, deviled eggs, and a shrimp tower. As I told the *Post*, "Nothing that's squishy, drippy, or red." The secret sauce is Duke's mayonnaise, the ingredient that will make anything taste Southern.

The centerpiece of any Kentucky Derby party is the mint julep, the bourbon-based drink served in authentic silver mint julep cups. For backup, I also serve my family recipe for General Lee's artillery punch. Let the drinker beware. It's called *punch* for a reason: The guest who drinks too much will definitely be down for the count. I serve it in punch cups, which are smaller than glasses. Follow this recipe, and a good time will be had by all.

General Lee's Artillery Punch

3 teaspoons fresh lemon juice

2 cups superfine sugar

1 pint bourbon

1 pint cognac

1 pint dark Jamaican rum

3 bottles good-quality champagne

• Mix alcohol with lemon juice and sugar and let sit in the refrigerator for twenty-four hours to mellow it out. When ready to serve, pour over a block of ice in a punch bowl and top with thinly cut slices of orange and small strawberries. The rest is history!

The book was successful, and I think the ideas at its core never get old—just like me.

Mario's health started failing in 2016, and he had to move to a care facility. It occurred to me that although we were close friends and travel companions for decades, I had never seen the interior of his apartment—no one had. He displayed it in *Architectural Digest* in 1992 and then closed the door for the next twenty-six years.

One day, I picked him up at his apartment building to accompany him to a doctor's appointment. He realized that he had forgotten his wallet, so we dashed upstairs to retrieve it. He opened the door just a crack and slipped in, inadvertently giving me a quick peek at what was inside. "Heavily layered" is the polite term for the interior's chaos. I didn't see much, but Mario wasn't kidding when he called himself a hoarder.

He worried that if anyone was allowed to clean, something might get moved, and he'd never be able to find it in the piles of fabric, furniture, and collectibles that filled the space. He also worried that strangers might steal from him, although how they would find valuables in the clutter (or how *he* would even know anything was missing) was a mystery. For these reasons, he eschewed help, maintaining that "dust is a protective covering for the furniture. I like it in big balls."

Mario offered other insights about his unique approach to housekeeping and personal maintenance. He claimed to wash his Brooks Brothers shirts in the dishwasher alongside the plates, a novel approach to laundry that I would not recommend.

The last time I got to see Mario, he was in the hospital, hooked up to all kinds of machines. His doctor confided that he couldn't eat or drink, so he was failing. I sensed that he recognized me and hoped that he could hear what I was saying. I told him how important he was to me and talked about all the wonderful places we had been, the people we'd met, the extraordinary things he had done, and the experiences we shared. Most of all, I wanted him to know how much it all meant to me—how much *he* meant to me. I finished by saying I would come back in two weeks, then paused, hoping he would acknowledge my heartfelt message.

He looked at me and said, "Will you check the sofa on your way out and see if that's the right print?"

I couldn't imagine a more Mario response. Even at the end, he was all about the work. He died shortly after, on October 15, 2018.

Two years later, the auction house Sotheby's paid homage to Mario's more-is-more style by offering many of his hoarded items— nearly one thousand—at a blockbuster sale. Buyers could score his famous chintz chairs, cabbage ceramics, and dog paintings (his ancestral portraits, he liked to say), and bring home some of his magic. The fact that the sale pulled in $7.6 million (two and a half times the estimate) proved that Mario's allure was just as strong in the afterlife.

I cochaired a luncheon Sotheby's hosted in Mario's honor, and Martha Stewart and Carolyne Roehm, fellow Mario fans, were at my table. Then, I attended the auction and bought one of the beautiful antique dog paintings in his collection (Brooke Astor had one by the same artist) just for auld lang syne.

Mario had so much stuff that Stair Galleries also staged a sale of his seemingly endless trove of collectibles. For all the antiques, artwork, and decorative objects, one of his most beloved treasures was nowhere to be found.

I wonder what happened to Harold?

Twenty-One

*S*outhern *Charm* and Bravo's other hit shows don't exist in a vacuum. They're constellations in the Bravo universe, and the overlord of this realm is Andy Cohen. I have a soft spot for Andy. He's whip-smart, affable, and entertaining, even when he's being outrageous. I've read every one of his books, and there's a reason why they're bestsellers. They're good!

When I signed my contract for *Southern Charm*, it didn't specify that I had to appear in the popular cast reunions that close every season, so I decided I would never attend one. They're brutal replays of all the drama I didn't want to live through the *first* time. If I have something to say, I say it during filming—whatever pops into my head at the time. And I'm truthful. I don't feel the need to be cross-examined after the fact.

Quite frankly, I think reunions are beneath me, and my absence says more than my presence ever would.

For the first couple of years, Andy asked Whitney, "Where's your mother?" hoping I might change my mind and appear on his show, *Watch What Happens Live*. In *Southern Charm*'s third season, Bravo announced that they had held a contest to name the best actress on reality television . . . and I'd won.

Of course I had to make my debut on *Watch What Happens Live* to accept my award. In my previous lives, I have won awards for my academic achievements, philanthropic pursuits, and efforts on behalf of historic preservation. On this occasion, I was presented with the Susan Lucci Award for Best Performance in a Reality Show, and it was given to me by none other than Susan Lucci herself. Susan, if you recall, was famous for having been nominated for nineteen Emmys for her performance on *All My Children* before she finally won, so I'm not sure if my award meant that I was a success or a failure.

In either case, Susan was delightful. I happily accepted my prize and thanked Whitney for putting me on the show. I also thanked Andy for not making me come to the reunions.

I'm happy to appear on *Watch What Happens Live* because Andy has always been a gentleman and treats me like a queen. I know I'm in good hands *and* that he will make me laugh. He may ask tough questions, but they're never mean-spirited, and they're usually a little silly so I can give equally silly answers, and we all have a good time.

As for reunions . . . you'd think that at my age, I'd know *never* to say never. I happened to be in New York when Bravo scheduled the reunion celebrating *Southern Charm*'s tenth anniversary. Ten Years! I decided to make an exception just this once and agreed to make a brief appearance. They surprised me by turning the enormous stage into a copy of my house, complete with the staircase. Everyone was very nice, and it was fifteen minutes of fun. Of course, I didn't get into the weeds about the cast's, shall we say, complicated relationships.

I'm all in for BravoCon, the annual convention and ultimate experience for Bravo fans because it's a chance to engage with "Bravolebs" from their favorite shows, including *The Real Housewives*, *Below Deck*, *Vanderpump Rules*, *Project Runway*, *Million Dollar Listing*, *Shahs of Sunset*, and, of course, *Southern Charm*.

The first BravoCon took place in New York in 2019 and offered three days of panels, parties, screenings, immersive photo opportunities, and a special edition of *Watch What Happens Live*, filmed before the largest audience in the show's history.

It's a lovefest, and the fans are amazing. They go crazy when they spot their favorites from a show and carry on as if they've come face-to-face with the Beatles or Taylor Swift. I've had fans burst into tears when I stood next to them for a selfie. One sweet fan showed up wearing a caftan from my collection. I think anyone who says it isn't fun is lying because the people are friendly, nice, and appreciative, and all of that is positive—a real ego boost. I haven't had anyone throw eggs at me . . . yet.

It's also fun to meet the stars from the other Bravo shows. Bravo hosted a cast luncheon on the first day of the convention, and everyone was there. Thankfully, André, who had vast experience, taught me the best way to navigate a big party. At one event we attended, I made the mistake of suggesting we "go mingle."

He looked at me as if I were crazy and said, "Honey, we don't mingle. They come to *us*."

I have followed his advice ever since then, and BravoCon was no exception. I sat at a table, and sure enough, the people I wanted to see found me. I watch *Below Deck*, so I was delighted to meet Captain Lee. We became good friends, and when he and his wife came to Charleston, I hosted a party for them and invited the cast from *Southern Charm*.

For some reason, Whitney refuses to go to BravoCon. I think he would enjoy it, and I'm hoping to persuade him to come with me in the future.

By 2020, I had settled into a comfortable routine of filming and enjoying my real life when, suddenly, in March, a curtain descended, and everything came to a halt. COVID. What a strange time in our history. Whitney was with me in Charleston when the virus hit. He had come to visit and was on the verge of renewing the lease on his house in Los Angeles. Luckily, he hadn't gotten around to signing, or he would have been saddled with a house he couldn't use for three years.

He stayed in Charleston, and we formed our own little pod with Michael and the dogs. We were fortunate to have indoor and outdoor space. Still, fear weighed heavily on us, just like everyone else. Our goal each day was to avoid catching the virus, no matter what lengths we had to go to protect ourselves.

Anyone who has seen me in action on a plane knows that I'm a germaphobe in the best of circumstances. COVID prompted me to institute NASA-level precautions. At the very least, we wore masks and gloves, but I even ordered an infrared machine that promised to zap bacteria. Deliveries were exhausting because I felt compelled to wave my magic infrared wand over every surface, a problem exacerbated by the fact that we were in a COVID delirium and shopping became a full-time job.

We ordered *everything*. Maine lobsters and Joe's Stone Crabs? Why not? How about some key lime pie? We were so afraid of running out of food that we were always thinking about our next meal—and the one after that. We stocked up on reserve supplies of toilet paper (or "comfort paper," as Michael calls it) and Veuve Clicquot. My nightly martini became the "quarantini," a nod to being housebound. We all developed a layer of protective padding.

My female friends remember our panic when we realized that trips to the beauty salon were not an option. Personal upkeep is a slippery slope, requiring serious attention to hair, skin, teeth, nails, and whatnot. The biggest battle is the one waged against gray hair. Once again, Michael demonstrated his ability to do anything by turning himself into *Monsieur Michael* and taking charge of my hair coloring. The gray didn't stand a chance when he wielded his brush; I have the picture to prove it.

During the pandemic, I found an app that upended all my previous thinking about cosmetics and beauty routines. I had listed what I considered to be my favorite products in my previous book. Then, I discovered Yuka, a mobile app that scans product labels and analyzes how healthy—or unhealthy—they are. I was shocked to see the chemicals and toxins in my go-to brands. I could slather myself with creams that were hazardous or switch to something safe. I instantly chose the latter. Now, I don't buy anything without checking on Yuka first.

The saving grace of living in lockdown was that I had an exciting new project. Home Shopping Network approached me with an idea—so many people admired my personal style and the decor of my home. Could I develop a product line featuring the kinds of items New York socialites buy for thousands of dollars but reconfigured with the magic of modern technology and materials to be affordable? "The Everyday Luxury Collection," high style without the high price tag.

I appreciate beauty and quality, but I also love a bargain, which is why I'm often seen trolling the aisles at Costco. I also worked with Mario, whom I consider to be the greatest decorator of the past two centuries, for thirty years and learned a lot from him. I was certain I could offer products with pop and style for the right price. All I had to do was look around me; inspiration was everywhere.

What did I love? Wrapping myself in soft blankets, sleeping on pretty sheets, adding whimsical touches to my home—maybe something unusual I picked up in my travels—and my perennial favorite, caftans.

I could spend my entire life in a caftan. When envisioning a line, I had to think about the shape. I like them to hug the body, so I had them sewn inside the border, which is more formfitting. I decorated them with fringe or embroidery to make them festive. I've spent a ridiculous amount of money on caftans over the years. The ones featured in my HSN collection looked like they cost $3,000, but we charged only $100, and that was the whole idea—to get the look and the quality at an affordable price.

When I decided to make sheets and comforters, I was inspired by the 1940s films I watched on Turner Classics Movies. The bedrooms are lavish and glamorous, with silk everywhere. I had these extravagant boudoirs in mind when I designed gorgeous, lush comforters and matching shams that look like silk but are made from more practical and inexpensive fabrics.

And here's the big secret about sheets that I learned from the manager of the Ritz Hotel in Paris. I always thought the higher the thread count, the better the sheet, but it's not true. Six hundred thread count sheets are heavy, and because they're so tightly woven, they're harder to clean. But sheets with a thread count of three hundred are light and breathable. I followed the manager's advice and produced sheets with a lower thread count, and they were everything I wanted them to be—comfortable, luxurious, and pretty.

I stand by my previously stated theory that couples should sleep in separate bedrooms because mystery can be a strong aphrodisiac in a relationship. I always did, even on the boat. But I recognize that it's not always possible, so I designed a pillow to communicate the evening's agenda in the boudoir—on one side, the word *Tonight*. Flip it over, and on the other side, the words *Not Tonight*. I think that says it all.

I also looked to my antiques for inspiration. For example, I have an enormous old Italian mirror that cost $35,000. I sent a photograph to my artists and asked if we could make it smaller, look as good, and keep it at a reasonable price. They fabricated it with modern materials, it looks fantastic, and it sells for $300. To be clear, I never copied the objects I was inspired to reimagine. I paid homage to them and made them affordable.

Creating the collection was a blessing during the interminably long days of COVID, but making personal appearances on HSN when I couldn't leave the house was definitely a challenge. It was me, myself, and my iPad, with my home as my showroom. I couldn't travel to the HSN studio or have a crew on hand because it was still dangerous to get close to people.

Initially, I may have felt a little destabilized by the do-it-yourself aspect of the filming, but as I got comfortable with the process, I realized there's not much difference between selling a million-dollar painting and a thirty-dollar wrap because good salesmanship means leading by example. When I was an art adviser and extolled the virtues of a Hudson River painting to a prospective collector, I spoke from the heart and explained why *I* thought it was valuable or a good acquisition. I did the same with my products, demonstrating how I used them and explaining in a very personal way why I thought others would like them, too. I had a few Vanna White moments, but it was fun to model and tell stories.

We had great success with the collection—everything sold out— and I genuinely enjoyed doing it, especially because I was described as an entrepreneur instead of a socialite. I earned that promotion because I worked so hard.

Later, when we resumed filming the show, *and* I started writing this memoir, I found it difficult to devote the requisite time to developing the products, so I had to stop. But I enjoyed everything about my foray into retail and would love to do it again.

I had another exciting new relationship in the works. No, not with a man, but with a spirit. The founders of Highclere Castle Gin asked me to be their brand ambassador. I was very enthusiastic about stepping into that role because I could combine my love of everything British with my love of everything gin, the finest gin.

Highclere Castle is a familiar sight to anyone who has watched Downton Abbey because it is the home of the Crawleys, the fictional family at the center of the series. In real life, Highclere is owned by Lord and Lady Carnarvon, who have turned the estate into a working farm where they grow botanicals, including juniper, one of the recipe components for gin.

Adam von Gootkin, the owner of Highclere Castle Gin, approached me because he wanted a brand ambassador who was passionate about gin, entertainment, and elegance. Well, I'm all three, so it came naturally to me to share my favorite cocktail recipes on Instagram and extoll Highclere's virtues.

People probably think I'm a dedicated alcoholic because the martini glass is an extension of my hand on *Southern Charm*. But I'm actually very discriminating, and I can honestly say that Highclere is a superior gin—infused with lavender and citrus—that elevates martinis to a new level. I should know—I've been drinking them my whole life. Cheers!

Beauty Edition

What is your beauty routine, and how has it changed over the years?
The biggest change is that I now pay more attention to the health
of my skin, the largest organ in the body. My first wake-up call was
when I checked the Yuka app and discovered that the high-priced
cream I used for years contained toxins. Now I check everything. I
use products by Augustinus Bader because they're all rated highly for
safety and results.

Another change in my routine is that I've added alternative reju-
venation therapies, like NAD infusions. NAD (Nicotinamide ade-
nine dinucleotide) is a coenzyme in our cells that diminishes as we
get older. It can be boosted with patches and infusions, and I think
it's the fountain of youth. I also do red-light therapy. And I follow
Dr. David Sinclair of Harvard, the foremost authority on longevity,
for his suggestions about supplements.

I posted a story on Instagram showing how I organize my skin
care and makeup products. I highlighted a few, like La Prairie, which
I've used for years. I arrange them according to their function—
grouping foundation, contour, concealer, blush, et cetera—and
they're all displayed on my dressing table. My favorite lipstick is by

Yves Saint Laurent, but I've been wearing it for so long they don't make it anymore. Fortunately, I have two tubes squirreled away. I collect products by Florasis because they look like little jewel boxes—I think I buy them for the packaging.

It looks like a lot, but then I need a lot!

Best makeup tip?
Having a good set of brushes and using the right brush for the proper application makes all the difference. Karen, my makeup artist, recommended Morphe x Ariel brushes, and they work beautifully.

How do I get hair that looks like yours?
Obviously, nobody my age is a natural brunette. But I think if you start out with brown hair or whatever your original color was, you should continue with it. I have friends who went from brown to blond, and it never looks right. For products, I buy my shampoo at Whole Foods—their 365 brand is highly rated and has no toxins.

Twenty-Two

W e were still in the throes of COVID in February 2021 when something terrible happened. This is what I remember and what I was able to piece together after the fact. We had a perfectly ordinary evening—Whitney was home, and Michael made dinner. The following day, Michael woke up in his cottage feeling under the weather but dressed and came to the main house to let the dogs out. Suddenly, he felt faint and started to lose consciousness. As he fell to the floor, he pulled the phone down with him and managed to press the "All page" button.

"Call an ambulance," he said into the speaker. "I'm having a stroke."

I was asleep upstairs but woke up when I heard his panicked voice and immediately dialed 911. Whitney also heard Michael's page, raced downstairs to help, and put a pillow under his head. By the time I got to the kitchen, the ambulance was pulling out of the driveway to rush Michael to the hospital.

When the doctors examined him, they confirmed that he had suffered a stroke, an acute spinal cord infarction, otherwise known as a spinal cord stroke. It was a rare condition, one I had not heard of before, and it left Michael with paraplegia, meaning paralysis of the legs and lower back. The news of his condition—and the terrible uncertainty of his future—was devastating. How could this have happened to him when everything had been fine the day before?

We couldn't be with him at the hospital because of COVID restrictions, which was terrible because we didn't want him to go through this alone. We weren't even sure what *this* was. Could he recover? What kind of help or support did he need? And where was the best place to get it? There were more questions than answers.

Our family doctor brought him whatever he needed. And Cameran's husband, Dr. Jason Wimberly, looked in on him. But the godsend in the situation came from, of all places, *Southern Charm*. Karen Thornton, who did hair and makeup for Bravo, told us she was friendly with Martha Shepherd, whose family founded the Shepherd Center in Atlanta. Specializing in treatment and rehabilitation programs for patients who have experienced strokes and spinal injuries, Shepherd was one of the most sophisticated facilities in the world—and had what appeared to be a mile-long waiting list of applicants.

I called Martha, who turned out to be a fan of *Southern Charm*. She had seen Michael on the show and wanted to help. She arranged for him to come to the center immediately. There, he began his long, arduous journey to recovery. First, surgery, then physical therapy and lessons in how to adjust now that his stroke had radically changed his life. Every stage was hard—physically and emotionally—but Michael approached his treatment with the best, can-do attitude. His determination was so great that he learned how to maneuver his wheelchair into a specially equipped van and drive.

Something wonderful happened when we posted news of Michael's condition. Fans of the show rallied, sending messages and gifts to express their concern. Our dear friend (and Michael's greatest champion) Luzanne Otte set up a dedicated social media account to enable well-wishers to connect with him, and friends and fans rallied to show their support and follow updates about his recovery. Their messages meant so much to Michael, who joked that he was the focus of a special-ops campaign, "Operation Heal the Butler."

After a few months, Michael moved to an assisted-living care facility in Sarasota, Florida, where he could be close to his family and make new friends.

The house wasn't the same without him. The dogs missed him—I swear they had their own language—and he was especially close to Peaches. I could search for another butler, but I would never find another Michael. I mean, I was shocked by the whole thing because he had been with us for eighteen years. My longest marriage lasted fifteen years, so Michael was the most stable and long-lasting relationship I've ever had. He was an important part of our family, someone I trusted, respected, and genuinely enjoyed.

Life is uncertain—you never know when it's going to change, so you have to savor every moment every day and appreciate the people who are important to you.

That year, 2021, became more of an annus horribilis when Lon, Whitney's father, died in August. He was diagnosed with leukemia and passed away a few weeks later, which was a terrible shock to all of us. Lon was a fabulous man, and I adored him. Even after we divorced, we always talked, and there was never an acrimonious word between us. Every once in a while, we'd argue about who would get Whitney for Christmas—as if he were a toddler instead of a grown man—but our conversations were always pleasant. I'll remember him as a wonderful father and a lovely human being, and I'm thankful that he and Whitney were always close.

Eventually, we resumed filming the show, although we had to comply with numerous social-distancing regulations because of

COVID, including having a nurse on the set, submitting to constant testing, and keeping a safe distance away from one another.

When life seemed to be returning to normal, I planned a Christmas visit to New York. Georgette scheduled a festive week of dinners, Broadway shows, and a visit to a spa for a hyperbaric oxygen therapy session that promised to promote new skin and blood vessels, which was exactly what we needed after becoming physical wrecks during lockdown.

COVID also erased time and blurred the edges of life—just getting through the day seemed like an accomplishment. The distance between the impulse to check in with a friend and actually making that call could be days, weeks, or even months. I felt out of touch and was eager to see my friends.

Of course I would make plans to see André. We had spoken several weeks before my trip, and he complained about not feeling well and thought he might have the flu.

Then, when I arrived in New York, the Omicron variant exploded, and it seemed everyone had COVID . . . again, even Hugh Jackman, the star of *The Music Man*, which meant we couldn't see the show. We quickly realized that we couldn't see any show or go anywhere. We were back in the bubble, fearful of getting sick, so Georgette and I spent the entire vacation wearing our masks, walking around the block, ordering takeout, and watching television. I might as well have been in Charleston. I decided I'd call André when I got home.

Two weeks later, on January 18, 2022, André passed away after suffering a heart attack. He was only seventy-three.

I regret not making that call.

"I live alone. I'll die alone. I climbed up alone, and I'll go down alone." That was André's somber assessment of his life, but what he accomplished was spectacular—the barriers he broke, the talent he mentored, the indelible mark he left on culture, and not just fashion, the wisdom and wit he shared, and the laughter.

On May 20, 2022, SCAD hosted a tribute to André in Savannah. I believed André was watching from somewhere—whichever afterlife was more fun and where the angels or devils were better dressed—because he'd never miss the opportunity to hear the tidal wave of praise coming in his direction. I also knew *exactly* what to wear.

I heard his voice in my head, "*Don't be wearing that cat dress.*" Well, I *did* wear the cat dress, partly to annoy him and partly to remember his impassioned opinions and deep current of affection that ran through our friendship. I also wore it when I appeared in a documentary about André's life, guaranteeing that my first encounter with André in the afterlife will be a quarrel about that dress.

Rihanna paid a sweet tribute to André at the 2023 Super Bowl when she appeared in a voluminous red sleeping bag coat designed by Alaïa. André was often seen in a similar one by Norma Kamali, one of the items included in the sale "The Collection of André Leon Talley" at Christie's on February 12. Prospective buyers could view and bid on André's treasures, including caftans, Louis Vuitton luggage, jewelry, photographs, and art. In the catalog, his possessions looked as if they belonged to a king. He *was* a king.

How I miss my fabulous friend.

Twenty-Three

⸺ ⸺ ◆ ⸺ ⸺

I don't know about you all, but after these past several years of the
pandemic, I just want to have fun and be silly. Besides, what could
go wrong at a dog wedding?" Famous last words. I posted this message
on Facebook because I wanted to explain my motivation for hosting a
wedding for my dog, Peaches, and Shep's dog, Little Craig, on *Southern Charm*. Yes, any sane person might "paws" before uniting two dogs
in holy mutt-trimony, but life had been so dark for so long that we all
needed a party and a good laugh. I also wanted to use the occasion to
raise money for an animal rescue organization I supported.

Besides, Little Craig had sullied poor Peaches's reputation by
getting too close, so the honorable thing—a shotgun wedding—was
in order. It was an excuse to call a caterer, break out the champagne,
put on a shiny caftan, and party like it was 2019. The only problem was that weddings bring out the worst in the men of *Southern
Charm*. Even when the "groom" is a small dog, they somehow see
themselves walking down the aisle, and panic sets in.

Shep unpacked every phobia he's ever had about marriage. Austen, the best man, balked at standing next to Madison, the maid

206 · PATRICIA ALTSCHUL

of honor, because there was too much fear-of-commitment history between them. Whitney expressed his anti-matrimony sentiments by playing a screeching, heavy metal rendition of "Here Comes the Bride" on his guitar and giving everyone the finger for a finale.

On top of that, one of the canine guests pooped, *and* it rained. With such an inauspicious start, it's no surprise that the marriage didn't last.

On another episode of *Southern Charm*, I thought it would be fun to dispel the notion that I'm Charleston's version of *Driving Miss Daisy*—that I've spent my entire life looking at the world from the back seat of a luxury vehicle. I want to go on record as having been a pretty crackerjack driver in my day. When Whitney and I lived in Georgetown, I had a silver Mercedes built like a tank, and I had no problem zipping it around the city. Whitney learned to drive with it, and I never worried about him being safe because it was like an army vehicle.

That car had quite a history. Whitney always had a job when he wasn't in school, and he did not work in glamorous places. One summer, he worked at a women's hospital cleaning the operating rooms, probably the most disgusting job he ever had. Another summer, he delivered pizza and had to drive the "tank" and put a pizza sign on top. He would stop a block before the delivery address and walk the rest of the way because he was too embarrassed to pull up in an oversize Mercedes.

I drove that car for thirty years until I moved in with Arthur, and he took over the wheel. He owned cars, but they were clinkers, so he preferred the Mercedes. Arthur, bless his heart, was the worst driver in the world. He smoked a cigar while he drove, so we had to leave the windows open, and I had this secret fear that if the car rolled over, I'd be decapitated. An accident wasn't out of the question because Arthur was easily distracted. "What's that?" he'd say, looking in the distance at something only he could see. Every ride was an adventure. And did I mention that the car was so old that it didn't have seat belts?

Eventually, we traded the Mercedes for a newer model and hired a driver. Then Michael drove me wherever I went. After Michael got sick, I wondered what it would be like to drive again, but Whitney refused to let me test my skills in his car. He said that I hadn't driven for a zillion years and that, at my age, I shouldn't be driving anyway, which is probably true.

I did the only reasonable thing: As soon as Whitney went out of town, I asked Shep to teach me how to drive Whitney's car, and we filmed our excursion for an episode of *Southern Charm*.

Our problems began in the driveway. Whitney's Rolls-Royce has a peculiar key, and we didn't know how to start the car, which was an inauspicious start. Fortunately, Randy, our temporary butler, was there and figured it out. Getting the car through the gate was tricky—as soon as I turned onto the street, I almost ran over someone riding a bicycle—then I noticed that streets seemed to have gotten a lot narrower since the last time I drove.

I think I was going about three miles an hour, and I drove up on the curb at least once. Shep wasn't the calmest companion. He yelled a lot. Then, as we reached a more populated area, I found myself surrounded by groups of students from the local college who ignored every traffic law and kept their eyes glued to their cell phones. Enough! I traded places with Shep and let him drive home.

What did I learn? If I had an emergency, I could probably drive myself somewhere. But I was happy to go back to being Miss Daisy. It was safer for me . . . and everybody else.

Ironically, many accidents happen at home, and in my case, in my own bedroom. This a cautionary tale. I woke up one morning at five. Still not fully conscious, I threw back the covers and popped out of bed in the dark. The next thing I knew, I was flat on my back on the floor, in excruciating pain. There was no one I could call for help because Whitney was in Europe. My housekeeper was coming later that morning, but that was hours away. Somehow, I managed to crawl back to the bed to wait for her.

On this of all days, I had locked the door to my bedroom, and my housekeeper couldn't get in. I called a locksmith, hoping he would come quickly. When we got through that crisis, my doctor rushed over to examine me. By this point, I couldn't move my back, and the pain was still intense. He arranged for me to go to the emergency room at the hospital for a CAT scan and an MRI. Then, he explained to me that the seemingly simple act of getting out of bed quickly is actually very dangerous.

Everyone, regardless of their age, should do *this*, he said. Before standing, turn on the light when you first awaken, and sit with your feet over the side of the bed for a moment because your brain and senses haven't adjusted to your new physical state. When you're lying flat, your blood is going a certain way, and if you stand up too fast, your body will not be able to catch up, and you may faint.

Now, a warning?

I wish I had known the correct way to get out of bed before my mistake landed me in serious trouble. I also learned there was another factor. Like everyone else, I had gained a few pounds during COVID, which I worked hard to lose. But after I got back to my pre-Covid weight, I neglected to adjust my blood pressure medication, so the dose was too high, and likely low blood pressure contributed to my sudden lightheadedness and fall.

Whatever the reason, the tests revealed that I had a compound fracture of the vertebra, and there were two things I could do—either lie flat in bed for an indeterminate period of time and let the bones heal naturally, or try a new treatment, which consisted of an injection of a concrete-like compound into my vertebral column.

Concrete in my spine? Well, screw *that*, I thought. All my friends who have undergone back surgery or some sort of invasive back treatment ended up being in constant pain. I decided I would rather have Mother Nature as my partner.

Not that healing naturally would be easy. I couldn't get out of bed, and when I was in bed, I couldn't even roll over. I needed a nurse to help me with everything. Whitney found one in the most unlikely place . . . at a funeral. Thomas Ravenel's father had died, and Whitney and his friends from the show went to the service to pay their respects. He met Mr. Ravenel's nurse at the funeral and followed up with a call, which is how I ended up with Paul, who turned out to be a real blessing.

I couldn't make any movement that involved using my back, which turns out is *every* movement. Paul was by my side from eight in the morning to eleven at night, helping me through the stages of recovery, from bedrest to wheelchair to walker. I took anti-inflammatories instead of painkillers and focused on physical therapy.

The simplest tasks were arduous—we had to get a special chair to position me at the sink so my hair could be washed. Fortunately, in addition to being a health care professional. Paul was a good soul who helped me with my skin-care routine and makeup, and he became proficient at holding the magnifying mirror and handing me my cosmetics in the right order. Why should I look like a total mess just because I couldn't bend my back? And I still wore nice lingerie, so I didn't have to look as bad as I felt.

My condition was fragile (I had to beware of my overenthusiastic dogs, especially Monty, who might knock me over), so I had to ask Whitney to host my annual gentlemen's dinner on the show, which was a shame because I'd planned quite an event. My inspiration for the theme came from a beautiful favor I had saved from my dinner with Prince Charles at Buckingham Palace. It was a painted paper fan with calligraphy detailing the menu for the evening. I had decided to re-create the experience of dining at Buckingham Palace, complete with a retinue of footmen serving the guests.

It might have been a pearls-before-swine moment for this "bro" crew, but my thought was that maybe an elevated meal would encourage elevated behavior. I'm sure *Southern Charm*'s producers, including Whitney, were hoping for the exact opposite.

Whitney did his best to bring my fantasy version of a British banquet to life in our dining room, but the cast was a little resistant. They wanted to know why there were so many footmen. They had no complaints about the food, probably because it was red meat.

Since I was confined to my bed of pain in another part of the house, I wasn't there to watch *if*—or, more accurately, *when*—the meal went south, as they inevitably do. Later, I learned the confirmation that re-creating the menu from Buckingham Palace had done nothing to inspire royal behavior. I hope the footmen weren't shocked.

How long will I be stuck in my room? I wondered. Taking my age into account, my doctors predicted I would be out of commission for a long time, and the fear was that I would never get back to who I was before the injury. But I *never* take my age into account and pushed myself to get better.

When I could walk on my own, I worked with a physical therapist, But I also tried all kinds of alternative treatments—peptide shots, NAD patches, and red-light therapy, which is supposed to promote recovery by increasing the production of mitochondria, the body's cells' energy sources.

I must have done something right because a year later, I was back to my old self and could run up and down the stairs.

I had to give up wearing high heels because I think that's kind of asking for trouble. As a result, there are a lot of sad and lonely shoes in my closet. They've been replaced by ballerina flats and Rothy's, which I love because when I step in dog poop, I can throw them in the washing machine, something you can never do with a sequined Jimmy Choo.

Eventually, I felt like my former self, although perhaps a little more contemplative. Mortality is not something we like to think about, especially our own mortality, but I thought about it more and more after my accident, and I had concerns. When I kick the bucket, who would take care of Whitney? He's an only child who just lost his father, and then I had this injury. It seemed like life was slipping away.

I want him to have a family, but whenever I ask if he's met someone, he tells me it's not that easy to find the right girl and that you can't rush these things. Why not? I mean, I always rushed into marriage. You have to take risks! And I want him to get married *now*, or at least get engaged—which my father did thirty times. I don't know why Whitney can't get started.

I'm hopeful because I've seen a change in him recently. He's talked more about settling down, and I think it's because his career has really taken off. You know, before, when he made documentaries, it was feast or famine. Now, he's produced three shows on television, including *Southern Charm*, *Southern Charm New Orleans*, and *Southern Charm Savannah*. He's sold two more TV shows, is working on three others, and has just done some big deal in China, so I don't think he's worried about career stability.

Whenever he's ready, I set aside four engagement rings—my grandmother's, my mother's, and two from my first two husbands—if he wants them. You can never have too many engagement rings.

I was also sad about Michael. I desperately needed a new butler, but it was hard to find anyone like Michael, who was irreplaceable in so many ways. Thankfully, we had Randy, our temporary butler, helping us. Poor Whitney was going to kill himself if he heard me ring my little bell one more time.

I had to delay seeing Michael in person, first because of the restrictions imposed on care facilities when we were in and out of COVID, and later when our shooting schedule kept me in Charleston, but I looked forward to doing so and kept in touch with him on FaceTime. We filmed one of our calls on the show so our viewers could see him, too. I wanted us to have an upbeat activity, so Whitney and I asked Michael to walk us through the steps of making his famous martini. He loved demonstrating his expertise, and we ended the call with a toast.

It was a bittersweet moment. As wonderful as it was to see Michael and slip into our usual banter, the call reminded me of his absence and all the people we'd lost—Lon, Mario, André—dear ones whose presence was missed. It was a shot in the heart, and the camera caught me wiping away tears.

I finally saw Michael right before Christmas 2023 in Sarasota, Florida. He was in good spirits then and showed me how he maneuvered his wheelchair into a specially equipped van and drove. We had a great lunch, laughing and talking about old times. I watched him drive off and thought how miraculous it was that he could go places and enjoy his family and friends in Florida.

Little did I know that it was the last time I would see him. Michael was in hospice, and he said he would prefer I not visit because his condition was deteriorating, and he didn't want me to see him that way. We continued to keep in touch by phone or text and had a long conversation in September 2024. When I asked how he was doing, he told me that he was dispirited because he was too sick to use his wheelchair. It was getting harder—even impossible—to do anything that gave him pleasure, and he didn't want to continue living that way. He needed my help. Would I look into the possibility of assisted suicide in Switzerland for him?

It wouldn't be my choice, but I respected his wishes. He fought that great fight, and it just wore him down. With a heavy heart, I called a friend who knew more about the subject than I did and tried to gather some information. Meanwhile, Florida was hit by Hurricane Helene, and I was concerned. I kept calling Michael's phone to see if he had been evacuated from the nursing home. Two days later, my phone rang with a call from Michael Kelcourse, but it was his stepmother.

"I have his phone," she said. "He's had another stroke, and he can't speak." Michael was in terrible shape.

His birthday was coming up on October 13, so I asked my followers on social media to send him their good wishes, hoping that cards would raise his spirits. More than three hundred people reached out to him, and his nurses read every message to him.

A short time after that, his stepmother called again. She said, "I guess you know why I'm calling." Michael had passed away. I was so upset to hear the news, but it was what he wanted, and he no longer had to suffer. With a heavy heart, I posted a tribute to him.

In Loving Memory of
MICHAEL KELCOURSE

It is with great sadness that we announce the peaceful passing of our beloved Michael, who left us yesterday morning in Sarasota. More than just a devoted butler, he was a trusted friend, confidant, and member of our family for over 20 years.

Michael's time on *Southern Charm* endeared him to many, as his humor and kindness quickly made him a fan favorite. Over the past two weeks, he was deeply touched by the incredible number of cards and well-wishes from fans. I've been told there were hundreds, and they brought him immense joy during his final days.

I will be devoting this week to remembering Michael. I know he meant so much to so many of you as he did to us. He will be greatly missed.

I wish I could tell Michael about the thousands and thousands of comments that appeared on my Instagram after my announcement. People thanked me for bringing him into their lives. One person said, "He was classier than I'll ever be, and I learned so much from him." Another wrote, "He was a bright light in this dark world. I can only imagine the way he made your life shine!" *Wonderful, dedicated, kind,* and *exceptional*—these were the words people used to describe Michael. He was all that and so much more.

Ask Me Anything...

Are you dating anyone?

I had a lovely relationship with an old friend a few years ago, a gentleman who was a philanthropist. He had been married to one of my best friends, and after she passed away, we started spending time together in Palm Beach. I really enjoyed his company. Sadly, he developed throat cancer and died a few months later. I'm too busy for a beau right now, but who knows what may happen in the future.

What's the secret to having a fun life after sixty?

It's the same "secret" that makes life fun after twenty, thirty, forty, or any age, really. Be an active, curious person, and always keep learning. I think it's important to cultivate younger friends and stay open to new experiences. I know some people my age who claim to be bored, but that's because they don't embrace change. Even learning how to do something like social media, which requires mental gymnastics if you weren't born with a cell phone in your hand, can be good for you. I came to Charleston to retire and eat bonbons, but now I'm busier than I ever was when I was younger.

What advice would you give to your younger self?
Have more husbands! If I'd had more energy, I might have had two more.

Looking back, is there anything in your life you wish could change? Any regrets?
I don't have one regret. I think regrets are a waste of time.

Epilogue

~~~~~~

I n the early days of *Southern Charm*, Bravo offered a featurette on the website called "Patricia's Corner," where Whitney asked me to weigh in on various topics—for example, what's my rule to determine when someone's had enough to drink? My answer? "When they cannot walk up the stairs in high heels, that's my rule for men *and* women." I'm never shy about speaking my mind, and we had fun doing it.

In this epilogue, I'm reviving "Patricia's Corner" to spill the tea on some misconceptions about me that have come up on and off the show.

First, the ridiculous idea that I'm just pretending to be Southern because I was born in Florida. For all the naysayers who are clearly map-challenged, Florida is, in fact, in the South. In fact, it's about as South as you can get without hitting the Atlantic Ocean. Florida definitely considered itself Southern during the Civil War because it was the third of seven states to secede from the Union and form the Confederacy. And I'm double Southern because in addition to being born in Florida, I was raised in Virginia. I think this is a "bless her heart" moment.

This leads me to another misconception that pops up like the undead in the Bravo universe. I have trouble writing the words. *Did I ever have a romantic relationship with Michael?* No . . . God, no. The relationship between an employer and a butler is completely professional and built on trust and mutual respect. Period. Please don't ask again.

Then, there's the deranged *Southern Charm* hanger-on who offered the low-rent psychoanalytic theory that I have been hard on Kathryn Dennis because she reminds me of myself at her age. Retire your couch, Dr. Freud, because your diagnosis is entirely wrong.

When I was twenty, I was deeply invested in my academic career. I was also happily married to a successful executive in the financial world, and while I worked on my graduate degrees, I often helped my husband with his Harvard Business School case studies. I took many tests when I was a student, but never one--let alone *two*—to determine paternity. Kathryn is who she is, and I wish her well, but we have absolutely nothing in common.

And stop speculating about what plastic surgery I've had. The answer is none. If you look at my neck, you'll know that I haven't had a facelift, but it irritates me that people think I have. I take very good care of my skin and I welcome the help of Botox. But the secret of eternal youth—or looking younger than my age—was passed on to me by my mother, who said to stay out of the sun or at least wear a hat and gloves to protect yourself. I still wear a hat when the sun is strong. And if I can believe the Internet chatter whenever I put up a picture of myself, it works!

The next canard is about Whitney. Does he sit at home and play his guitar all day? Whitney has a good time showing his lighter side on the show, but that's far from who he is—a successful producer with an incredible work ethic. In addition to producing *Southern Charm* and its spin-offs, he's hard at work on the documentary *Mrs.*

America, a scripted comedy, *Family Office*, and several other shows. He develops projects and oversees every detail of bringing them to life, from casting to sales. I wish he were home more, but he's usually working in Los Angeles, attending a film festival in some faraway place, or at meetings in international cities. He's also a philanthropist who supports numerous charities.

And how about the myth that I ensnared three rich husbands so I could be a lady of leisure and live off their sizable bank accounts? I think the correct term is gold digger. If you've read this far in my memoir, you know none of that is true. I've always worked, and *leisure* was rarely a word in my vocabulary. As an academic, I taught multiple classes each semester. As an art adviser, I bought and sold priceless paintings and earned more money than I could possibly spend. By the time I married Arthur, I had several rewarding and lucrative careers behind me and transitioned to philanthropy. I was an active member of the Director's Circle at the Metropolitan Museum of Art and was honored to be named a "fellow in perpetuity" for my service to the museum. I also served on the Rockefeller board of Historic Hudson Valley. In 2012, I received the Woman of the Year Award for Philanthropy in New York and a congratulatory letter from US senator Chuck Schumer.

Make no mistake, appearing on a reality television show is work, hard work. The schedule, from shooting scenes to additional green screen segments, is demanding, and I've been doing it for ten seasons.

I thank Whitney for the opportunity he's given me because somebody my age usually is stuck with similar old bats playing cards or going on trips together. *Southern Charm* allows me to be with people of all ages, especially young people, and it's enormously fun for me to be in that environment. Where else would I receive an honor like "The Golden Crappie Award for Outstanding Achieve-ment and Being One of the Only Cast Members Who Hasn't Made Out with @krollthewarriorking," otherwise known as Austen Kroll? I think it's important to have a sense of humor—and gratitude—for the unexpected places life takes us and the gifts we enjoy every day.

I'm grateful for my pets and treasure my time with them. Some-times, I prefer them to people. Dogs and cats have always been an important part of our family, and they usually outnumber us. I'm sure the neighbors think we're running a kennel. In addition to Lily and Chauncey, we've had Siegfried and Roy, my spirited Pomera-nians; Monty, the Lagotto (a breed that specializes in truffle hunt-ing, although he's unlikely to find any in Charleston); Smoochie, Whitney's dog from California; and little Peaches, who was always Michael's favorite.

Soon after Michael died, we had to say goodbye to Chauncey, our sweet pug who won everyone's hearts. At the age of nine, Chauncey was diagnosed with spinal degeneration, and his neurolo-gist explained that there was no cure. First, he had trouble walking, so we carried him everywhere. Then, he had difficulty breathing. It was heartbreaking to watch him suffer, and as painful as it was, we had to let him go. Whitney went to McDonald's to pick up Chauncey's favorite food—a Double Big Mac and fries—and Chauncey sat on a cushion like the prince he was and wolfed it down. When he was finished, our vet eased his transition into the next world. I'm grateful that he had a peaceful passing.

After we resigned ourselves to the idea that Michael would not be coming back to live in the cottage, Whitney took it over and redesigned it, creating a place to entertain on the first floor and an office on the second floor. His extensive guitar collection is housed there—which makes me *very* happy.

Actually, Whitney is my landlord. Recently, I sold the Isaac Jenkins Mikell house to his trust because it was smart estate planning. When I kick the bucket (no time soon, I hope), he won't have to deal with probate and all the bureaucracy that comes with it. As the owner of the house, he takes his responsibilities very seriously. I happily gave him the list of handymen, plumbers, electricians, gardeners, and whatever you call the people who clean the gutters, and it's a huge relief to me that he's in charge of everything and doing such a good job.

Now, I can enjoy the house for the pleasure it gives me and for the happy memories that echo in every room—memories of dear houseguests, lively dinners, fabulous parties, and tranquil moments on the piazza—yes, with a cocktail in hand.

I've had a *charmed* life. I've attended formal dinners in the White House, Buckingham Palace, and Versailles. I've traveled on mega yachts and the Concorde. However, I'm equally happy at McDonald's or getting a Costco hot dog. And I know all the good barbecue places.

I never really think about last words because I'm not going *anywhere*, but I always like *having* the last word. This quote, which has been credited to the great wit Dorothy Parker says it all . . .

I like to have a martini,
Two at the very most.
After three I'm under the table.
After four I'm under my host.

Acknowledgments

I have been blessed in so many ways, and the greatest blessing of all is my son, Whitney Sudler-Smith. My thanks to him and to my dear family and the many friends who have enabled me to enjoy such a wonderful life. And I extend my deepest appreciation to my friend and co-author, Deborah Davis, whose eloquent writing has brought my story to life.